KU-747-985

Cooking for Friends

Cooking for Friends

Prue Leith

NEW ENGLISH LIBRARY

For Donald and Angela

First published in Great Britain in 1978 by The Hamlyn Publishing Group
Limited

First NEL Paperback Edition February 1983

NEL Books are published by
New English Library,
Mill Road, Dunton Green,
Sevenoaks, Kent.
Editorial office: 47 Bedford Square, London WC1B 3DP

Photoset in Great Britain by South Bucks Photosetters, Beaconsfield
Printed by Cox & Wyman, Reading

British Library C.I.P.

Leith, Prudence
  Cooking for friends.
  1. Entertaining   2. Cookery
  I. Title
  641.5′68   TX731

ISBN 0-450-05371-7

Contents

Useful Facts and Figures

Notes on metrication

In this book quantities are given in metric and Imperial measures. Exact conversion from Imperial to metric measures does not usually give very convenient working quantities and so the metric measures have been rounded off into units of 25 grams. The table below shows the recommended equivalents.

Ounces	Approx g to nearest whole figure	Recommended conversion to nearest unit of 25
1	28	25
2	57	50
3	85	75
4	113	100
5	142	150
6	170	175
7	198	200
8	227	225
9	255	250
10	283	275
11	312	300
12	340	350
13	368	375
14	396	400
15	425	425
16 (1 lb)	454	450
17	482	475
18	510	500
19	539	550
20 (1¼ lb)	567	575

NOTE: When converting quantities over 20 oz first add the appropriate figures in the centre column, then adjust to the nearest unit of 25. As a general guide, 1 kg (1000 g) equals 2.2 lb or about 2 lb

3 oz. This method of conversion gives good results in nearly all cases, although in certain pastry and cake recipes a more accurate conversion is necessary to produce a balanced recipe.

Liquid measures. The millilitre has been used in this book and the following table gives a few examples.

Imperial	Approx ml to nearest whole figure	Recommended ml
¼ pint	142	150 ml
½ pint	283	300 ml
¾ pint	425	450 ml
1 pint	567	600 ml
1½ pints	851	900 ml
1¾ pints	992	1000 ml (1 litre)

Spoon measures. All spoon measures given in this book are level unless otherwise stated.

Can sizes. At present, cans are marked with the exact (usually to the nearest whole number) metric equivalent of the Imperial weight of the contents, so we have followed this practice when giving can sizes.

Oven Temperatures

The table below gives recommended equivalents.

	°C	°F	Gas Mark
Very cool	110	225	¼
	120	250	½
Cool	140	275	1
	150	300	2
Moderate	160	325	3
	180	350	4
Moderately hot	190	375	5
	200	400	6
Hot	220	425	7
	230	450	8
Very hot	240	475	9

Useful facts and figures

Notes for American and Australian users

In America the 8-oz measuring cup is used. In Australia metric measures are now used in conjunction with the standard 250-ml measuring cup. The Imperial pint, used in Britain and Australia, is 20 fl oz, while the American pint is 16 fl oz. It is important to remember that the Australian tablespoon differs from both the British and American tablespoons; the table below gives a comparison. The British standard tablespoon, which has been used throughout this book, holds 17.7 ml, the American 14.2 ml, and the Australian 20 ml. A teaspoon holds approximately 5 ml in all three countries.

British	American	Australian
1 teaspoon	1 teaspoon	1 teaspoon
1 tablespoon	1 tablespoon	1 tablespoon
2 tablespoons	3 tablespoons	2 tablespoons
3½ tablespoons	4 tablespoons	3 tablespoons
4 tablespoons	5 tablespoons	3½ tablespoons

An Imperial/American guide to solid and liquid measures

Solid measures

IMPERIAL	AMERICAN
1 lb butter or margarine	2 cups
1 lb flour	4 cups
1 lb granulated or castor sugar	2 cups
1 lb icing sugar	3 cups
8 oz rice	1 cup

Liquid measures

IMPERIAL	AMERICAN
¼ pint liquid	⅔ cup liquid
½ pint	1¼ cups
¾ pint	2 cups
1 pint	2½ cups
1½ pints	3¾ cups
2 pints	5 cups (2½ pints)

NOTE: WHEN MAKING ANY OF THE RECIPES IN THIS BOOK, ONLY FOLLOW ONE SET OF MEASURES AS THEY ARE NOT INTERCHANGEABLE.

Introduction

When I last wrote a cookery book on the subject of 'entertaining' things were very different. It was still reasonable to recommend a bottle of Château Margaux with the grouse (it was still reasonable to recommend the grouse!) and I could even assume that on special occasions a helper could be hired or bullied into backstage duties.

There must still be households where a parlourmaid brings in the claret, and where expense is no object, but this book is not for them. True, I have included some extravagant and luxurious recipes, for high days and holidays when the cook wants to pull out all the stops, but there are far more recipes for food that won't break the bank, and that can be managed with a minimum of last-minute effort. So the emphasis is on the informal. But, at the risk of sounding pedantic, I must say that the friendliest and most casual parties, that seem effortless and easy to both hosts and guests, need planning. Unless you have the style and confidence to give your friends the children's toothmugs for glasses, unless you can be truly relaxed when the booze runs out, unless you are so competent that you can cook the dinner with your kitchen full of merry mates, then some forethought and preparation is what you need.

The obvious and golden rule is to keep it simple. One good dish is a better idea than a three-course meal if you haven't anyone who will help, and you've a room full of people to feed.

Do as much as you can well before the party – even if your chosen dish cannot be cooked in advance, if everything else is done the cooking will be easy. And I mean *everything* else: lay the table, put a clean towel in the loo, put the drinks/wine/ice out, get the kitchen completely clear of washing up and debris, even assemble the cooking implements, dishes and food you will need. Have you ever seen a restaurant chef's table just before the 'service' begins? On the table is a clean board; beside it lie the chef's knives; to one side are dishes of washed watercress, chopped parsley, lemon segments; the half-made sauces are kept hot in a bath of warm water; the food has been prepared as far as possible – Chicken Kiev has been rolled in egg and crumbs and chilled, just ready to plunge into the deep fat which is already heated to the correct temperature; the rack of lamb

11

is lying in its roasting tin, trimmed, buttered and covered with herbs and seasoning, and the oven is blazing hot. Above the range serving dishes are warm and within reach: when the first order comes the chef has no need to move more than a yard, and there is no risk of delay as he chases about looking for a tea towel or a wooden spoon.

So take heart and do as the professionals do. I don't mean it *matters* if your friends have to wait another 5 seconds, or 5 minutes, but hunting for things flusters the cook, whereas if all is going like clockwork he or she will be riding high, elated and pleased at his or her own efficiency.

A word about menu planning: it is very easy to choose three dishes you like, and serve them one after the other without thought of their combined effect. Of course there are no rigid rules, but try to avoid two fishy things in one menu, two meaty things, two creamy things, two boozy things and so on. If you are serving baked eggs for starters, don't use eggs again in the pud (so a soufflé and a custard in the same meal is out). Also, consider the texture and the colour of the food: for example, soup, followed by chicken fricassée, followed by a mousse is too soft and mushy; veal in a cream sauce, served with cauliflower and Jerusalem artichokes is altogether too white – it cries out for something crisp and green, or bright orange like carrots.

The recipes in this book are split up into Cheap, Not-So-Cheap and Simply Extravagant sections, each containing a chapter on Starters, Main Courses and Puddings. There are also chapters on Vegetables and Salads. Of course no one is bound to cook a whole meal from one section, or indeed to have three courses at all. A fairly grand main course is often the better for following a cheap and easy starter. And many of the starters, in more substantial quantities, would make excellent main courses, or one-and-only courses for informal parties. So to use the book: decide whether the meal is to be a no-holds-barred extravagant orgy, a simple supper, or whatever. Then find your main course and work from there, adding salads, vegetables, starters or puds as you think fit.

Now, the thorny question – can I cook it, then freeze it? The answer is probably yes, but on the whole I'm against it – at least for party food. There is is no doubt that most dishes (the exceptions being cakes, breads and so on) lose something of texture, if not taste, in a domestic freezer. And unless you are really quite an experienced freezer cook and slavishly obey the rules about setting the freezer at maximum, wrapping well, excluding air, making sauces with special thickening flour instead of household flour (because if you don't, the sauce comes out watery), thawing slowly, and so on, you are likely to have a disaster on your hands. I have a freezer, but it is mostly filled with produce from the garden, and children's suppers – Shepherd's

Pie and Fish Cakes freeze at least satisfactorily enough to satisfy the family. The saving of time by bulk cooking, and the peace of mind derived from knowing no one will be reduced to cornflakes because I'm not there to cook, make the slight sacrifice in gastronomic quality a bargain. But I really could not bear to freeze a boned stuffed turkey, cooked, though I might well freeze it raw (see recipe page 184). However casual we are with our friends we do make an extra effort if they are to eat with us, so why jeopardise the results with the risk of shreddy dry meat, mushy texture or a panic to get an unyielding block of stew thawed? I'd rather do something quick and simple that can be fixed between getting home from work and my bath (Blanquette of Veal? Fish Kebabs with Bacon?), or something that can be made the day before and kept in the fridge (almost anything in a sauce, or something good and moist – Carbonnade, Coq au Vin, Curry, Bollito, Moussaka, for example).

About quantities: the recipes in this book, by and large, are for four or five people. If you are serving 20 people, it stands to reason that you will make four times the stated quantity (or maybe that you will make the recipe four times – it is often better to cook in smaller, more easily controlled quantities than to struggle with a vast mass of ingredients). But should you be cooking for 40 people, you will not need eight times the original recipe. It is an odd fact, but a true one, that the more people there are the less per head they will eat. As a rough guide, allow 225 g/8 oz of meat for each person for parties of under 12 guests, 200 g/7 oz for between 12 and 30 people, 175 g/6 oz for between 30 and 60, and 150 g/5 oz for over 60 people. This law of diminishing need is particularly true of salads. I suppose the reason is that not everyone likes 'rabbit food', as my husband calls anything raw, and if there are 30 people in the room you can be sure a certain proportion won't touch it. But if you are catering for six you cannot risk it – you might just have six rabbits on your hands.

What to drink?
I'm a wine addict and get thoroughly disgruntled if I have to spend the whole dinner on spirits or orange juice. But even worse is to have to play with really horrible 'Brewers' Burgundy' – that over-vinegary, over-sweetened brew too often sold in supermarkets by supermarket managers who never touch the stuff, and simply say, when asked for advice, 'This sells well, madam'. One answer to the whole fraught question of buying wine, if you don't know what you want, is to go to a respectable, preferably small, wine merchant and ask *his* advice (wine merchants are a lot less stuffy and wine-snobby than some of their customers), telling him what you are eating and how much you want to spend.

Introduction

The other answer is to forget all the pompous jargon and learn a little bit about it. So many excellent cooks, who can very easily tell you if the cabbage is sour or nasty, or recognise that pickled beetroot is both sweet and sour, become paralysed with fright when asked to taste a wine, and end up doubting their own judgment. If the wine tastes vinegary to you, it probably *is* vinegar, or very nearly. This is not to say that a wine expert doesn't have a highly trained palate and knows a vast amount more about the subject than we do. A professional tea-taster may be able to detect a single leaf of Darjeeling in a packet of Ceylon, but that doesn't mean the rest of us don't know if tea is too weak, too strong, or stewed. If you want to learn a little about wine, and know nothing now, buy a simple book on the subject and slowly drink your way through the cheaper end of your wine merchant's shelves.

But to get back to what to drink at dinner. The much-ridiculed 'white with white meat, red with red meat' rule is not so stupid after all. Of course there are some white wines, good strong white burgundies, for example, that have enough power to stand up to the hefty taste of roast beef, but red wine is generally stronger or 'bigger' than white. In fact, at the risk of over-simplifying, I would say that *any* good red wine will go with *any* red meat, and *any* good white wine, provided it is dry, will go with *any* fish or chicken dish. (I exclude sticky sweet ones, like Sauternes and the German *beerenauslese* because they are for feast days when you are having a wine with the pud *as well*). To say you must have Chablis for shell-fish or claret for lamb is crazy. The Italians eat plenty of shell-fish and plenty of lamb, and wouldn't dream of importing French wines to go with them. They drink Italian wines, but probably white with the fish, and red with the lamb.

One last thing. I do wish we could somehow magic the angst out of party giving: if a party goes well, if the food is good, and so is the company, the conversation and the drink, feeding friends can be the most satisfying and gratifying of pleasures. But if something goes wrong, if the ice melts or the soufflé sinks or the wrong number of people turn up, it really should not matter. No one is going to starve, no one minds all that much if he has to eat off a tea plate or share a beer.

The simple fact is that your friends have come to see you, not to give marks for the excellence or otherwise of your cooking, or to write notes on the wine for the Good Food Guide. And so the more they see of you, relaxed and able to concentrate on them, the better. The best party-givers are the ones who seem to be one of the guests, not some maid-of-all-work, constantly leaping up to empty ashtrays or fill glasses, too distracted to hear a word of conversation, too nervous to enjoy a mouthful. Besides, what is the point of it all if the chief organiser, cook and skivvy doesn't have a good time too?

Cheap...

Starters

ARTICHOKE SOUP

METRIC/IMPERIAL
675 g/1½ lb Jerusalem artichokes
50 g/2 oz butter
1 onion, sliced finely
½ clove garlic, crushed
600 ml/1 pint creamy milk
600 ml/1 pint chicken stock *or* water and a stock cube
salt and freshly ground black pepper
chopped chives

Peel the artichokes and leave them soaking in water until you are ready for them. They will discolour if you leave them in the air.

Melt the butter in a heavy-bottomed saucepan, and gently cook the onion until it is soft and transparent-looking, but not coloured. Then add the crushed garlic and stir for a few seconds. Slice the artichokes into the pan and stir well. Put on a lid and continue cooking gently for about 10 minutes, giving the pan an occasional shake.

Add the milk and chicken stock, season well and leave the soup to simmer for a further 20 minutes. Try not to boil it as it just might curdle. When the artichokes are soft check the soup for seasoning; plenty of salt and pepper are needed.

Push the soup through a sieve or liquidise it very well in a blender. Just before serving sprinkle with the finely chopped chives.

SERVES FOUR

DUTCH BEAN SOUP

METRIC/IMPERIAL
2 large onions, chopped
100 g/4 oz minced pork
50 g/2 oz fatty bacon, minced
salt and pepper
½ teaspoon rubbed sage
1 stick celery, chopped
2 leeks, chopped
40 g/½ oz butter
350 g/12 oz brown beans *or* red kidney beans
soaked overnight, boiled, and mashed
1.5 litres/2¾ pints good beef stock
curry powder
ground cloves

Combine half the onion with the pork and bacon and season well.
Add the sage and make into small balls.

Slowly cook the rest of the onion, the celery and the leek in the
butter until they are very soft but not browned. Add the mashed
beans and stock. Heat, stirring, then add the meat balls. Cook for 30
minutes and add a pinch each of curry powder, cloves, salt and
pepper.

SERVES FOUR TO SIX

MUSSEL SOUP

Many people are nervous of mussels, thinking that they spell instant food poisoning. But they are perfectly safe as long as any broken mussels or dead ones are discarded before you begin. To tell whether a mussel is dead, tap it sharply against the side of the sink: it should close tightly. If it refuses to close, throw it away. Also throw away any broken mussels or any which, when all the others are cooked and have opened, refuse to open.

METRIC/IMPERIAL
1.15 litres/1 quart (or about 1 kg/2 lb) fresh live mussels
1 small glass white wine
450 ml/¾ pint water
1 bay leaf
bunch of parsley
sprig of thyme
1 stick celery, sliced
40 g/1½ oz butter
2 medium onions, finely chopped
40 g/1½ oz flour
450 ml/¾ pint milk
salt and freshly ground black pepper
ground nutmeg
150 ml/¼ pint single cream

Soak the mussels in fresh water to remove any sand. Scrub them well, removing the 'beards'.

Put the cleaned mussels into a large heavy-bottomed saucepan and add the wine. Put on the lid and, holding the saucepan in one hand and the lid with the other, shake over a fairly fierce heat tossing the mussels as you do, so that they turn constantly in the pan. After a few minutes of this all the mussels should be open.

Take them off the heat but do not throw away any of the juices in the pan. Allow the mussels to cool sufficiently to handle, then lift them from their shells, but keep all the shells. Pull off the rubbery band round each mussel and throw it away. Put the mussels aside, covering them to prevent them drying out. Pour the water into the saucepan on top of the wine already in it and add the bay leaf, parsley, thyme and celery. Put back all the shells. Bring the liquid to the boil and simmer for 10 minutes.

In another saucepan melt the butter and add the finely chopped onion. Allow it to cook until the onion is soft and transparent, but not at all browned. Stir in the flour and continue stirring over the heat for 1 minute. Draw the pan off the heat and strain in the liquid from the first saucepan. With a whisk or wooden spoon stir until the liquid boils, and thickens smoothly.

Add the mussels and the milk and cook gently, without boiling, for a further 4 or 5 minutes. Push the soup through a sieve or liquidise it in an electric blender. Add salt, pepper and nutmeg to taste and stir in the cream. Care should be taken not to boil the soup – the flavour will still be delicious but the velvety texture is half the pleasure of the soup, and this would be spoiled by curdling.

SERVES FOUR

LENTIL SOUP

METRIC/IMPERIAL
350 g/12 oz dried lentils
1.15 litres/2 pints ham stock, saved from boiling a bacon joint,
or if not available, use:
50 g/2 oz onion, roughly sliced
a small bacon bone *or* handful of bacon rind
or small chunk of bacon
1 bay leaf
1 chicken stock cube
handful of parsley stalks
1.15 litres/2 pints water
3 or 4 tablespoons cream
1 teaspoon finely chopped mint
small fried bread squares (croûtons)

Place lentils in a large bowl, cover with boiling water and soak for 2 hours. Rinse and transfer them to a large saucepan.

Cover with the ham stock. If no ham stock is available, put the onion, bacon or bacon rind, bay leaf, stock cube and parsley stalks in with the lentils and cover with the water. Simmer very gently for 45 minutes or until the lentils are mushy (the cooking time varies enormously according to the age and type of lentil). Liquidise or sieve the soup and return it to the pan.

Stir in the cream and reheat carefully without boiling. Just before serving add the chopped mint and the hot fried croûtons.

SERVES FOUR

MUSHROOM SOUP

This is the archetypal mushroom soup, enormously rich and absolutely delicious. It is best made with flat field mushrooms, but even the little white Paris mushrooms are good.

METRIC/IMPERIAL
50 g/2 oz butter
1 clove garlic, crushed
350 g/12 oz flat black mushrooms, roughly chopped
3 slices of white bread with the crusts cut off
1–1.15 litres/1½–2 pints good chicken stock
salt and freshly ground black pepper
nutmeg or ground mace
at least 2 tablespoons finely chopped fresh parsley
about 150 ml/¼ pint single cream

Melt the butter in a large heavy-bottomed saucepan, add the garlic and stir for half a minute or so and then add the chopped mushrooms. Turn them gently in the butter until they are slightly greasy, then put a lid on the pan and leave them to cook gently for 10 minutes or so. By this time they should be soft and mushy and the smell of cooked mushroom and garlic should be overpowering as you lift the lid.

Break the bread up roughly and add it to the mushrooms. Then add the stock and season with salt, pepper and a good pinch of nutmeg or ground mace. Bring the soup to simmering point while you stir it, and then simmer slowly for 10 minutes. Liquidise the soup in a blender or put it through a vegetable mouli or coarse-grained sieve. Return the soup to a clean saucepan, add the chopped parsley and the cream and heat carefully without boiling.

SERVES FOUR

GREEK LEMON SOUP

This soup cries out for toast, or hot Greek bread.

METRIC/IMPERIAL
1.15 litres/2 pints good chicken stock, absolutely fat free
50g/2 oz long-grain rice
juice of 2 lemons
2 eggs
salt and freshly ground black pepper
½ tablespoon chopped mint
½ tablespoon chopped parsley

Heat the chicken stock to boiling point and toss in the rice. Boil steadily for about 10 minutes or until the rice is tender. In a jug, mix the lemon juice and eggs together. Add a cupful of the hot stock to the egg and lemon mixture and beat really well. Take the soup off the heat and carefully pour in the egg and lemon.

Reheat the soup without bringing it anywhere near boiling point (the egg will curdle if you boil it). Taste the soup, adding salt and pepper as necessary. Just before serving stir in the mint and parsley.

SERVES FOUR

BRUSSELS SPROUT SOUP

METRIC/IMPERIAL
1 kg/2 lb Brussels sprouts
1 leek
50 g/2 oz butter
1 tablespoon flour
1.15 litres/2 pints chicken stock
1 tablespoon grapefruit juice
salt and pepper
pinch of nutmeg
2 tablespoons cream
FOR THE GARNISH
3 rashers streaky bacon

Wash the Brussels sprouts and chop them very finely. Thoroughly wash and finely chop the leek. In a large heavy-bottomed saucepan melt the butter and put into it the Brussels sprouts and the chopped leek. Stir the ingredients so that they are well coated in butter and set over a gentle heat to soften, covered with a lid. When the mixture is considerably reduced in quantity and is soft and mushy, stir in the flour. Add the stock and stir until the soup boils. Add the grapefruit juice and season with salt, pepper and nutmeg. Simmer for 5 minutes then push the soup through a sieve, or liquidise it in a blender. Stir in the cream.

Grill the streaky bacon rashers until crisp and brittle and break them up. Reheat the soup without boiling it, and scatter the bacon bits on top before serving.

SERVES FOUR

LEEK AND BACON FLAN

METRIC/IMPERIAL
FOR THE PASTRY
175 g/6 oz plain flour
good pinch of salt
90 g/3½ oz butter
1 egg yolk
2 tablespoons icy water
squeeze of lemon juice
FOR THE FILLING
15 g/½ oz butter
1 small onion, finely chopped
50 g/2 oz rindless bacon, finely chopped
1 large or 2 small leeks, well washed
4 tablespoons creamy milk
4 tablespoons single cream
1 whole egg and 1 yolk
25 g/1 oz strong Cheddar cheese, grated
salt and pepper

To make the pastry, sift the flour with the salt. Rub in the butter until the mixture looks like coarse breadcrumbs. Mix the egg yolk with a little of the icy water and the lemon juice and stir it into the flour with a knife. Using first the knife and finally a lightly floured hand, mix to a firm dough. (It may be necessary to add the rest of the water but don't do this immediately as the pastry should not be too damp – crumbly pastry is difficult to handle but it is much shorter and less likely to shrink during cooking.) Leave the pastry in the refrigerator while you make the filling.

Melt the butter in a heavy-bottomed frying pan and gently cook the onion and diced bacon together. When the onion is soft but not browned, shred the white part of the leek very finely and add it to the pan. Cover with a lid and cook until the leeks and onions have an almost transparent look. Remove from the heat. Mix together the milk, cream and eggs and into this tip the contents of the frying pan and nearly all the grated cheese. Season with salt and pepper – as both the bacon and cheese are salty, add the salt sparingly.

Take the green middle leaves of the leek and slice them finely until you have about 2 tablespoons. Dunk these in boiling water for 1 minute to soften, drain immediately and rinse under the cold tap to set the colour and stop any further cooking.

Set the oven to moderate (180°C, 350°F, Gas Mark 4). Roll the pastry out and line a 15-cm/6-inch flan ring or flan dish with it. Bake this pastry case 'blind'. To do this line the raw pastry case with a piece of foil or a double sheet of greaseproof paper and fill it with dried beans, lentils or anything heavy enough to hold the pastry flat. After about 15 minutes, remove the paper and the 'blind' beans and return the empty pastry case to the oven to dry out a little more – about 5 minutes.

Carefully pour the leek and egg filling into the pastry case and return it to the oven. After 15-20 minutes, when the custard filling is beginning to set round the edges, sprinkle the green leek shreds over the custard and stir carefully with a fork. Sprinkle the flan with the rest of the grated cheese and return to the oven. After a further 10 minutes the flan ring, if you are using one, can be removed to allow the outer edge of the pastry case to brown. Bake until the filling is barely brown on top and just set. Serve hot or cold.

SERVES FOUR

SALMON FISH CAKES

Salmon costs so much these days this recipe has no right to be in the Cheap Starters section. However, it does occasionally happen that there is a single portion of left-over salmon in the fridge, or a can on the shelf. But any fish will do.

METRIC/IMPERIAL
225 g/8 oz cooked mashed potato
225 g/8 oz flaked cooked salmon *or* 1 (212-g/7½-oz) can salmon
salt and freshly ground black pepper
15 g/½ oz butter, melted
squeeze of lemon juice
1 tablespoon chopped parsley
1 egg, beaten
FOR THE COATING
dried white breadcrumbs
beaten egg
oil for frying
parsley sauce

Mix the potato and fish together and season well. Stir in the melted butter, lemon juice, chopped parsley and enough of the egg to bind the mixture together so that it is soft but not sloppy. Allow to cool.

Flour your hands well and shape the mixture into flat fish cakes about 2.5 cm/1 inch thick. Dip each cake into beaten egg and then into the breadcrumbs making sure that both egg and crumbs cover the cakes completely.

Heat the oil in a frying pan and fry each fish cake until brown on both sides. Serve immediately with hot parsley sauce.

SERVES FOUR

PARSLEY SAUCE

METRIC/IMPERIAL
300 ml/½ pint creamy milk
1 onion, sliced
4 peppercorns
bay leaf
good handful of fresh parsley
25 g/1 oz butter
20 g/¾ oz flour
salt and freshly ground black pepper

Put the milk into a pan with the onion, peppercorns, bay leaf and the stalks from the parsley. Bring slowly to the boil and simmer for 10 minutes.

In another pan melt the butter. When it is foaming stir in the flour and cook gently for half a minute, stirring all the time. Draw the pan off the heat and slowly strain on the hot milk, stirring as you do so. Return the pan to the heat and bring to the boil, stirring continuously. Simmer the sauce gently for a few minutes while you chop the parsley leaves very finely. Add the parsley, taste the sauce and season as necessary.

If liked, a little more butter (about 15 g/½ oz) can be beaten into the sauce for extra richness. Alternatively a tablespoon of cream may be added.

MOULES MARINIÈRES

There is always great argument about whether this dish should have cream in the liquid or not. Please yourself.

METRIC/IMPERIAL
2.25 litres/4 pints fresh live mussels
200 ml/8 fl oz dry white wine
1 large onion, chopped
2 tablespoons chopped parsley
25 g/1 oz butter
25 g/1 oz flour
salt and freshly ground black pepper
2 tablespoons cream (optional)

Soak the mussels in fresh water to remove any sand. Scrub them well, pulling away the 'beards'. Discard any broken mussels or mussels that will not close when tapped lightly on the sink edge. Put the cleaned, still wet, mussels into a large saucepan and add the white wine, chopped onion and half the parsley. Put the lid on the pan and shake over gentle heat until all the mussels have opened. This will take 2 or 3 minutes. As soon as they are opened remove the pan from the heat.

Put the mussels into a warm serving dish and cover them to prevent them drying out while you make a sauce from the liquid in the pan. Mix the butter and flour to a paste. Put the cooking juices over the heat again and, stirring continuously, drop in small half-teaspoons of the butter and flour paste. Simmer for 10 minutes. Taste the liquid and add salt and pepper, cream if liked, and the rest of the chopped parsley. Serve the sauce poured over the mussels, or separately in a sauce boat.

In inexpensive seaside restaurants in France all the Moules Marinères ingredients (but without the butter/flour thickening) are put in a pan together, the whole lot shaken over the heat until the mussels are opened and then tipped into a large bowl for serving. I'm not sure they don't taste the better for the casual treatment.

SERVES FOUR

MACKEREL AND MUSHROOM STARTER

This dish can be served either as a hot or a cold starter. If it is served cold, quartered peeled tomatoes are a good addition.

METRIC/IMPERIAL
1 medium onion, finely chopped
olive oil for frying
1 clove garlic, crushed
1 large mackerel, cleaned, filleted and cut into chunks
225 g/8 oz mushrooms, sliced
1 tablespoon fresh, chopped savory or thyme
1 tablespoon tomato purée
lemon juice
salt and freshly ground black pepper

First fry the onion in a little of the olive oil until soft but not coloured. Add the garlic and the chunks of mackerel. Shake over a moderate heat until the mackerel is cooked. With a perforated spoon, lift the mackerel on to a serving dish. Put the sliced mushrooms into the frying pan with a little more olive oil if necessary. Add the chopped thyme or savory and fry fairly fast to brown the mushrooms. When they are sizzling and cooked stir in the tomato purée and a tablespoon of water. Tip the mixture on top of the mackerel chunks. Add a good squeeze of lemon juice and plenty of salt and freshly ground black pepper.

SERVES FOUR

LEMON AND SARDINE PÂTÉ

METRIC/IMPERIAL
225 g/8 oz canned sardines
225 g/8 oz butter *or* 100 g/4 oz each
cream cheese and butter
juice of ½ lemon
small teaspoon French mustard
salt and freshly ground black pepper
lemon leaves or sprigs of dill for decoration

Beat together the sardines, with their oil, and the butter (or butter and cream cheese) until well blended. Flavour with the lemon juice, mustard, salt and pepper and put into a small pâté dish, or into individual cocotte or ramekin dishes. Decorate with the lemon leaves or dill and chill the pâté well. Serve with fingers of hot toast.

This pâté is frequently served on a lettuce leaf in scooped-out lemon shells, which looks pretty and festive. It can be accompanied by black olives and garnished with a sprig of parsley.

SERVES FOUR

BRIOCHES WITH TUNA MOUSSE

METRIC/IMPERIAL
4 brioches, or very small soft bread rolls
1 (198-g/7-oz) can tuna fish
½ clove garlic, crushed
2 hard-boiled eggs, finely chopped
2 tablespoons soft butter
freshly ground black pepper
squeeze of lemon juice
few black olives, stoned

Cut the tops from the brioches or buns but keep them. Scoop out some of the soft bread from the bottom half of the buns.

Make a soft mousse by mixing together the tuna flesh (without its oil), the crushed garlic, hard-boiled eggs, soft butter, and enough freshly ground black pepper and lemon juice to give a good strong flavour. Spoon this mixture into the hollowed-out buns and put one or two olives into each. Replace the tops.

SERVES FOUR

CUCUMBER AND YOGURT MOUSSE

METRIC/IMPERIAL
1 large cucumber
100 g/4 oz full-fat cream cheese
2 tablespoons double cream
150 ml/¼ pint yogurt
salt and freshly ground black pepper
juice of 1 lemon
grated nutmeg
150 ml/¼ pint chicken stock
15 g/½ oz gelatine

Peel the cucumber and grate all of it except a small chunk to be used for decoration. Oil a soufflé dish or mould if you intend to turn the mousse out.

Beat together the cream cheese, cream and yogurt. Mix in the grated cucumber and season with salt, pepper, lemon juice and nutmeg. Put the stock into a small heavy saucepan and sprinkle the gelatine on to it. Leave for 10 minutes or so until it looks spongy.

Then warm it over a very gentle heat until clear and runny and stir briskly into the cucumber mixture. Turn the mixture into the mould or dish and chill in the refrigerator until set.

To turn out, run a knife round the edge of the mousse, invert a plate over the top, and turn the dish and plate over together. Give a sharp shake to dislodge the mousse. Use the remaining chunk of cucumber for decoration – perhaps in thin overlapping slices round the top edge of the mousse.

If a less coarse-textured mousse is required the ingredients can be blended together in a liquidiser before the addition of the gelatine.

SERVES FOUR

EGG MOUSSE WITH ANCHOVIES

The more anchovy essence you put into this dish the better it is in my opinion. The anchovy essence seems to give it an almost crab-like flavour. Of course, if you want a pure egg mousse just leave out the anchovy essence.

METRIC/IMPERIAL
2 tablespoons water
½ tablespoon gelatine
6 eggs, hard-boiled
6 tablespoons mayonnaise
3 tablespoons single cream
salt and freshly ground black pepper
cayenne
anchovy essence
1 egg white
TO DECORATE
12 anchovy fillets
radishes, a few small gherkins, and slices of cucumber

Put the water in a small heavy saucepan. Carefully sprinkle on the gelatine and leave for 10 minutes or so until it looks spongy. Lightly oil a soufflé dish or jelly mould if you intend to turn the mousse out when it is set.

Chop the eggs finely and mix them with the mayonnaise and cream and season with pepper and cayenne. Add as much anchovy essence as you like – I like a good tablespoon. Now taste the mixture and add more salt if necessary. Put the gelatine over gentle heat and warm it until clear and runny. Add this, stirring briskly.

Whisk the egg white until stiff enough to hold its shape, but not dry-looking, and fold it into the egg mixture too. Pour the mixture into the oiled mould or your serving dish. Refrigerate until set.

To turn the mousse out, run a knife round the edge to loosen it. Put a plate over the top, turn the plate and mould over together and shake.

To decorate, split the anchovy fillets lengthwise and use them to lattice the top of the mousse. Cut very thin rings of radish and gherkin and place them in the diamond-shaped spaces of the lattice pattern. Surround the mousse with thin slices of cucumber. If the mousse is not to be served immediately, salt the cucumber slices half an hour before using them, rinse and pat dry.

SERVES FOUR TO FIVE

Main Courses

BUBBLE AND SQUEAK

METRIC/IMPERIAL
450 g/1 lb buttery mashed potatoes
50 g/2 oz good dripping *or* butter
1 medium onion, sliced
1 leek, sliced
450 g/1 lb cabbage
salt and pepper
1 egg (optional)

Make sure that the potato is well seasoned and soft but not sloppy. Melt the dripping in a heavy-based frying pan and gently fry the onion and leek until they have a soft melted look, slightly transparent.

Meanwhile, shred the cabbage coarsely and plunge it into boiling water for 3 or 4 minutes or until it is just tender. Drain well and season with salt and pepper.

When the onion and leek are cooked mix all the vegetables together – potatoes, cabbage, leek and onion. Heat the pan again, adding a little more fat if necessary, and press the mixture into it, forming a flat cake. Fry over gentle heat until the underside is slightly browned, and the mixture is very hot.

If you want a neat cake that can be cut into slices when cold this is the time to add the egg: beat it with a fork in a small bowl and pour into the pan. It will run round the edges of the potato and set the mixture rather like a Spanish omelette. Flip the bubble and squeak over on to a warmed serving dish, or alternatively, serve straight from the frying pan.

SERVES FOUR

FRENCH CRÊPES OR PANCAKES

METRIC/IMPERIAL
FOR THE PANCAKES
100 g/4 oz plain flour
pinch of salt
1 whole egg and 1 egg yolk
1 teaspoon oil
150 ml/¼ pint milk
150 ml/¼ pint water
oil for frying

If you have a blender simply put all the ingredients into it and whizz briefly, but be careful not to let the mixture become bubbly. If you are preparing the ingredients by hand, sift the flour and salt into a large bowl and with a wooden spoon make a well in the centre. Into this drop the eggs and the oil. Using the wooden spoon, mix the mixture in the centre to a thin batter, gradually drawing in the surrounding flour and adding milk and water as you go, maintaining a thick creamy consistency. When all the flour is incorporated you should still have a little liquid left. Add this now. Whether you have made the batter by hand or in a blender it should now be left for 20 minutes or so to settle.

Grease a heavy pancake pan or omelette pan with a little oil (use a small piece of cloth or kitchen paper for this). When the pan is hot pour in about 2 tablespoons of the batter and slowly tilt the pan so that the batter evenly covers the bottom without being too thick. When the pancake has browned underneath, carefully turn it over and brown the second side.

Slide on to a tea towel or plate and keep warm while you make the rest of the pancakes. The number of pancakes you make with this mixture will depend on size and thickness.

MAKES NINE TO TWELVE

PANCAKE PIE

METRIC/IMPERIAL

8 pancakes (see French Crêpes or Pancakes recipe, page 36)
1 tablespoon beef dripping
450 g/1 lb minced beef
1 large onion, chopped
1 stick celery, chopped
4 rashers streaky bacon, diced
1 clove garlic, crushed
½ tablespoon flour
150 ml/¼ pint stock
1 tablespoon sherry *or* Madeira *or* Marsala
1 tablespoon tomato purée
pinch of thyme
chopped parsley
salt and freshly ground black pepper
1 (142-ml/5-fl oz) carton soured cream

Make the pancakes according to the recipe and leave them in the folds of a tea towel while you make the meat sauce.

Melt half the fat in a large heavy-bottomed saucepan and in it brown the meat well. With a perforated spoon lift out the meat and then fry the onion, celery, bacon and garlic until they are just turning brown, adding more fat if necessary. Return the meat to the saucepan and stir in the flour. Now add the stock and liquor (Madeira, Marsala or sherry) and bring to the boil, stirring all the time. Add the tomato purée, thyme, parsley and salt and pepper to taste. Simmer gently until the meat is tender and the sauce is reduced to a syrupy thick consistency. Be careful not to allow the bottom to catch. Check the seasoning – it should be fairly peppery and strong.

Allow the meat sauce to get cold. Take a serving dish with a good lip and put one pancake on the bottom. Spread this with a tablespoon of the now-rather-solid sauce and then put another pancake on top. Continue to sandwich pancakes and sauce together in a pile, finishing with a layer of sauce. Put the pancake pie into a moderately hot oven (190°C, 375°F, Gas Mark 5) to reheat and serve with soured cream spooned over the top at the last minute. A sprinkling of chopped parsley looks good too.

If this pancake pie is to be made and eaten in the same hour the pancakes can be kept hot in a gentle oven while the sauce is made, and then the hot sauce and pancakes can be served immediately.

SERVES FOUR

SPINACH AND CHEESE PANCAKES

METRIC/IMPERIAL
10 pancakes (see French Crêpes or Pancakes recipe, page 36)
1 kg/2 lb fresh leaf spinach
150 g/5 oz Mozzarella cheese *or* 50–75 g/2–3 oz
each cream cheese and Gruyère cheese
75 g/3 oz butter
450 g/1 lb mushrooms
lemon juice
salt and pepper
ground nutmeg

Make the pancakes according to the recipe and keep them wrapped in a tea towel until you are ready.

Wash the spinach and remove any coarse stalks. Put it, still wet, into a heavy-bottomed saucepan and cover with a lid. Cook over moderate heat, shaking the pan frequently, for about 3 minutes or until the spinach is much reduced in quantity and is soft and tender. Remove from the heat, drain, and press as much moisture out of the spinach as you can (pressing between two plates is a good way).

Slice the Mozzarella or Gruyère into as thin slices as possible. Melt half the butter in a frying pan. Slice the mushrooms into the butter and add a good squeeze of lemon juice. Cook them for 2 or 3 minutes, shaking the pan frequently.

Take an ovenproof dish with a good lip and into the bottom of it put one pancake. Spread it with a spoonful of the mushrooms. Put another pancake on top, and this time put a thin layer of sliced Mozzarella, or a layer of cream cheese spread thinly with a few pieces of Gryuère as well. Then another pancake. Mix the rest of the butter into the spinach, and season it well with salt, pepper and nutmeg. Use a spoonful of this for your next layer. Then another pancake and so on. Finish with a top layer of cheese.

Reheat the pancake pie in a moderately hot oven (190°C, 375°F, Gas Mark 5), removing it when the top layer of cheese is melted and just beginning to brown – about 15 minutes. SERVES FOUR TO FIVE

FISH PIE

METRIC/IMPERIAL
1 kg/2 lb fillet of haddock, whiting, cod or a mixture
450 ml/¾ pint milk
few parsley stalks
1 bay leaf
few slices onion
piece of celery
6 peppercorns
salt and pepper
25 g/1 oz butter
25 g/1 oz flour
1 tablespoon chopped parsley
2 tablespoons cream
4 hard-boiled eggs
little butter
450 g/1 lb buttery mashed potatoes

Lay the haddock in a roasting tin and pour over the milk. Add the parsley stalks, bay leaf, sliced onion, celery and peppercorns. Season with salt and cover tightly with foil. Put in a moderate oven (180°C, 350°F, Gas Mark 4) until the haddock feels firm to the touch and will flake easily with a fork. Carefully lift the haddock fillets out on to a plate and cover with the foil to prevent drying out while you make the sauce.

Melt the butter in a saucepan and stir in the flour. Cook, stirring, for half a minute and then draw the pan off the heat. Strain the cooking milk from the roasting tin into the saucepan and stir well. Add the chopped parsley, return to the heat and keep stirring until the sauce boils. Taste and season with more salt and pepper if necessary. Add the cream.

Chop the hard-boiled eggs roughly. Flake the haddock into a bowl, keeping the pieces as large as possible. Add the sauce and the chopped eggs. Mix well taking care not to mash the fish too much.

Butter a pie dish and turn the mixture into it. Cover carefully with the creamed mashed potatoes and mark the top in a lattice pattern with the back of a fork. Brush the potatoes with melted butter and brown in a hot oven (230°C, 450°F, Gas Mark 8) for 10 minutes before serving.

If the pie is to be reheated from stone cold it will need 25 minutes in moderate oven (180°C, 350°F, Gas Mark 4) rather than 10 minutes in a hot one.   SERVES FOUR TO FIVE

BREAM WITH SAGE AND ONION STUFFING

A whole baked fish is a rare treat, and sea bass, whole small haddock, and grey mullet are more and more difficult to find. But occasionally one can get a small sea bream or haddock.

METRIC/IMPERIAL
1 sea bream or haddock, about 1.75–2.25 kg/4–5 lb
FOR THE STUFFING
50 g/2 oz fresh white breadcrumbs
1 onion, finely chopped
1 tablespoon fresh chopped sage *or*
1 teaspoon dried rubbed sage
1 small egg, beaten
salt and freshly ground black pepper
butter
lemon juice

Have a fishmonger clean the fish and remove the scales but leave the head and tail intact.

Set the oven to moderate (180°C, 350°F, Gas Mark 4). Mix together the stuffing ingredients, taking care to season very well. Use this to fill the cavity of the fish. Lay the fish on a piece of buttered foil and brush all over with melted butter. Sprinkle well with the lemon juice and wrap the foil up around the fish enclosing it completely in a parcel. Lay it on a baking tray or in a roasting tin. Bake for 40 minutes–1 hour, depending on the size of the fish. It is cooked when a skewer will glide easily into the flesh.

The fish does not look very glamorous at this stage because, having been enclosed in a foil packet throughout its cooking, it has not been able to brown. But the purpose of the foil is to trap the flavour and the juices, and the fish will taste wonderful. However, if improved appearance is desired the fish can be served with a bunch of watercress at its head, or scattered with chopped parsley or garnished with lemon slices. Alternatively the top skin could be browned under the grill at the last minute.

Because the fish has been cooked in its own juices the flesh will be very moist, making a sauce unnecessary, but if liked a little melted butter mixed with lemon juice and perhaps some finely chopped onion is very good.

SPANISH OMELETTE

This is more of a potato and onion cake than an omelette as we normally know it. Very good cold on a picnic, or straight from the pan for lunch or a light supper.
Make the omelette in one large paella pan or frying pan if you can. Otherwise, use two frying pans, each containing half the ingredients.

METRIC/IMPERIAL
75 g/3 oz butter
4 medium mild Spanish onions, coarsely sliced
4 large potatoes, boiled
1 large clove garlic, crushed (optional)
6 eggs
4 tablespoons water
salt and freshly ground black pepper

Melt the butter in the frying pan and in it slowly soften the onions. This should take at least 20 minutes, the onions becoming greatly reduced in bulk, and transparent and soft before they turn colour. When they are ready add the potato, cut in slices. Turn the heat up slightly and allow both onions and potatoes to take in the butter. If garlic is used, put it in now and mix well.

Mix the eggs in a bowl with a fork and add about 4 tablespoons of water. Season well with black pepper and salt. Pour the egg mixture on top of the onions and potatoes and turn the heat under the pan right down. Shake the pan as the omelette cooks and occasionally lift one side to allow the uncooked egg to run underneath. The omelette is done when the bottom is browned (lift it with a palette knife and take a look) and the top is still moist. Serve direct from the pan, cut into large wedges.

SERVES THREE TO FOUR

KEDGEREE

METRIC/IMPERIAL
50 g/2 oz butter
150 g/5 oz cooked long-grain rice, weighed before cooking
350 g/12 oz smoked haddock fillet, cooked, skinned and boned
3 hard-boiled eggs, coarsely chopped
salt and freshly ground black pepper
pinch of cayenne

Melt the butter in a saucepan and add everything else to it. With a fork stir gently until very hot.

Kedgeree, if well buttered, will reheat in a cool oven (150°C, 300°F, Gas mark 2). Keep covered with foil and fork occasionally.

SERVES FOUR

HAMBURGERS

The whole secret of good hamburgers is good beef to begin with, and plenty of seasoning. A basic hamburger should simply be minced beef steak, with a small proportion of beef fat in it, salt and pepper. But variations are frequent, many people adding Worcestershire sauce, mustard, finely chopped onion, chopped herbs, and frequently rusk or other cereal binder to make the meat go further. This recipe seems to me the best. It makes 4 good-sized burgers.

METRIC/IMPERIAL
450 g/1 lb minced lean beef steak (shin or skirt are good,
rump or sirloin the best)
1 small onion, very finely chopped
2 tablespoons chopped parsley
plenty of salt and pepper

Mix the ingredients together using first a fork and then your hand. Shape the meat into thick rounds of absolutely equal size. They should not be too thin or they will dry up during cooking. Heat the grill at least 10 minutes before you need it. Grill the burgers steadily, turning them once only.

Depending on the thickness of the meat they should take about 5 minutes per side for rare, and 10 minutes for well done. Serve as they are with a salad or sandwiched in heated soft buns. Hamburgers are generally served with a selection of mustard, finely sliced raw onion, dill pickle (bought in jars) and tomato ketchup.

SERVES FOUR

MEAT BALLS

METRIC/IMPERIAL
FOR THE MEAT BALLS
450 g/1 lb minced beef
225 g/8 oz belly of pork, minced
50 g/2 oz fresh white breadcrumbs
1 medium onion, finely chopped
1 tablespoon chopped parsley
pinch of dried thyme
good pinch of ground nutmeg
salt and pepper
3 tablespoons milk
flour for rolling
bacon fat or beef dripping for frying
300 ml/½ pint beef stock
1 (298-g/10½-oz) can tomato soup
1 (142-ml/5-fl oz) carton soured cream

To make the meat balls simply combine all the ingredients and mix well. Using floured hands, roll the meat balls into even-sized balls (or flattish patties if you prefer) and fry them on all sides until brown in hot bacon fat or beef dripping. Lift them out of the fat and put into a clean saucepan.

Mix the stock and the tomato soup together and pour over the meat balls. Cover with a lid or foil and bake in a moderately hot oven (190°C, 375°F, Gas Mark 5) for 30 minutes or until the meat balls are cooked through. (If good quality steak was used the cooking time can be as little as 20 minutes but if cheaper meat was used they may need 1½ hours to become really tender.) Tip the meat balls and their sauce into a serving dish and spoon blobs of soured cream on the top. Very good served with rice or mashed potato.

SERVES FOUR

MIGHTY MEAT LOAF

This meat loaf can be eaten hot or cold, and is very substantial.

METRIC/IMPERIAL
5 rashers streaky bacon, with the rinds removed
350 g/12 oz minced beef
350 g/12 oz minced belly of pork
225 g/8 oz minced pigs' liver
100 g/4 oz fresh white breadcrumbs
2 onions, finely chopped
3 hard-boiled eggs, chopped
1 egg
1 tablespoon chopped parsley
1 tablespoon chopped chives
small pinch of rubbed sage
salt and freshly ground black pepper

Use the streaky bacon rashers to line a 1-kg/2-lb loaf tin or large pudding basin. Mix all the rest of the ingredients together. Taste for seasoning. (Many people dislike tasting raw meat, but it really is essential if an insipid meat loaf is to be avoided. In fact it tastes quite good!) Fill the loaf tin or pudding basin wth the mixture and cover with greaseproof paper or foil.

Stand the tin or basin in a roasting tin two thirds full of hot water and bake in a moderately hot oven (190°C, 375°F, Gas Mark 5) until the meat loaf feels firm to the touch and has slightly shrunk from the edges – about 2 hours. Alternatively, the meat loaf can be steamed in a steamer or covered saucepan half filled with water for about 2½–3 hours.

A spicy tomato sauce (see page 45) is good with this meat loaf if it is to be served hot.

SPICY TOMATO SAUCE

METRIC/IMPERIAL
1 (396-g/14-oz) can peeled tomatoes
1 onion, finely chopped
1 clove garlic, crushed
½ teaspoon dried oregano *or* a good teaspoon chopped fresh marjoram
good pinch of nutmeg
½ teaspoon cumin seeds *or* a good pinch of ground cumin
1 tablespoon tomato purée
1 teaspoon sugar
1 bay leaf

Simmer all the ingredients together until a syrupy consistency is
obtained, then push the sauce through a sieve. If it is liquidised in an
electric blender the tomato seeds will still be present but the sauce
will taste just as good.

OXTAIL STEW

METRIC/IMPERIAL
1 large oxtail, weighing about 1.5 kg/3 lb, jointed
2 tablespoons beef dripping
2 medium onions, sliced
1 medium carrot, peeled and diced
1 small turnip, peeled and diced
1 stick celery, chopped
bunch of herbs (bay leaf, sprig of thyme, sprig of parsley)
tied together with string
1.15 litres/2 pints beef stock
1 tablespoon ruby port
lemon juice
1 tablespoon flour, mixed to a paste with
1 tablespoon butter
salt and pepper
TO SERVE
chopped parsley

Wash the oxtail and trim off any excess fat. Pat the joints dry. Melt
the dripping in a heavy saucepan and fry the oxtail fairly fast until
well browned, lifting the pieces out as they are done. Fry the onions

until soft and brown all over. Then add the carrot, turnip and celery and turn them in the fat until they are softened slightly, and just beginning to colour. Put back the meat, add the bunch of herbs and stock and bring to the boil. Cover and simmer gently for about 3 hours, or until the oxtail is meltingly tender and will almost fall off the bone. During the cooking it is important to skim off the fat as it rises to the top.

Once cooked, lift the oxtail and vegetables on to a serving dish and keep warm. Skim the sauce again and put it back over the heat, adding the port and a squeeze of lemon juice. Drop small pieces of the flour and butter paste into the sauce, whisking steadily. When all the flour and butter mixture is incorporated the sauce should be slightly thickened. Now boil rapidly to reduce to a good rich gravy. Add salt and pepper to taste and pour over the oxtail joints. Sprinkle with chopped parsley before serving.

SERVES FOUR TO FIVE

CHILLI CON CARNE

METRIC/IMPERIAL
225 g/8 oz dried red kidney beans, soaked overnight
225 g/8 oz lean pork
225 g/8 oz lean stewing beef
2 tablespoons bacon fat
300 ml/½ pint beef stock
3 tablespoons red wine
1 onion, finely chopped
2 cloves garlic, crushed
½ tablespoon flour
½ tablespoon chilli powder
1 bay leaf
pinch each of cumin, turmeric, dried oregano
salt and freshly ground black pepper
TO SERVE
boiled rice

Boil the kidney beans for 1–2 hours in the water in which they soaked until soft, adding more boiling water if necessary. Drain.

Cut the meat into small cubes. Melt half the bacon fat in a heavy-bottomed saucepan and in it brown the meat, frying only a few pieces at a time and lifting them out as they are done. If the saucepan becomes dry and very brown add a little wine, water or beef stock and bring it to the boil, scraping the bottom of the pan with a spoon to loosen the brown sediment. Keep this liquid to add later – it will improve the flavour.

Place the browned meat in a heavy saucepan with all the stock, the wine and any juices from the pan. Fry the onion in a little more bacon fat and when it is soft and just beginning to turn colour add it to the meat. Add the garlic, cover the saucepan and bring to the boil. Simmer for 1 hour. In a measuring cup mix the flour and the chilli powder with enough hot juices from the pan to make a soft paste. Stir this into the saucepan and add the bay leaf, cumin, turmeric, oregano, salt and plenty of pepper. Cover again with the lid and continue to simmer until the meat is very tender – about another 1½ hours. Add the cooked kidney beans and reheat. Adjust the seasoning and serve with hot plain boiled rice.

This recipe is frequently made with minced beef or a mixture of minced beef and minced pork, but the cooking method is essentially the same. However, the final simmering will probably not need to be longer than 45 minutes.

SERVES FOUR

AMERICAN PORK AND BEANS

METRIC/IMPERIAL
450 g/1 lb dried haricot beans
225 g/8 oz salt pork *or* streaky bacon in 1 piece
225 g/8 oz fresh belly of pork
1 large mild onion, sliced
2 tablespoons tomato purée
2 tablespoons black treacle
2 garlic cloves, crushed
1 teaspoon dried English mustard
1 teaspoon chopped fresh sage
salt and pepper

Soak the haricot beans overnight but do not throw away the water. Soak the salt pork or bacon piece overnight if it is home-cured or very salty – otherwise don't bother.

Cut the pork and the bacon into 2.5-cm/1-inch cubes, discarding the rind. In a large casserole combine all the ingredients, including the water in which the beans are soaked. Season well and top up with more water if necessary – the ingredients should be almost covered by liquid. Cover the casserole and bake in a moderate oven (180°C,

47

350°F, Gas Mark 4) for 1½ hours, or until the beans are cooked and soft and the pork very tender.

If the dish is rather wet, containing too much liquid, lift out the solid ingredients with a perforated spoon, tip the liquid into a saucepan and boil rapidly until you have not more than 300 ml/ ½ pint left. Pour this over the solid ingredients and serve.

SERVES FOUR

PORK CHOPS WITH JUNIPER

METRIC/IMPERIAL

6 large loin of pork chops, including if possible the kidney
675 g/1½ lb potatoes, peeled and sliced
salt and pepper
1 tablespoon fresh chopped basil
1 tablespoon chopped parsley
1 clove garlic, crushed
12 juniper berries, crushed
veal or chicken stock

Trim the rind and most of the fat from the pork chops and pack them interspersed with layers of potato in a casserole. As you put in the ingredients season evenly throughout. Add the herbs, garlic and juniper berries with enough stock to barely cover the casserole and put on the lid.

Bake in a moderate oven (180°C, 350°F, Gas Mark 4) for 1¾ hours or until both potatoes and pork are very tender. At this stage the casserole will taste delicious but won't look very appetising. To improve its appearance either scatter some fresh chopped herbs on the top or brush the top lightly with butter and grill until brown.

EASY PORK PIE

METRIC/IMPERIAL
450 g/1 lb minced belly of pork
5 large basil leaves, finely chopped,
or 1 teaspoon rubbed sage
1 egg
50 g/2 oz fresh white breadcrumbs
salt and coarsely ground black pepper
175 g/6 oz puff pastry
(frozen and defrosted is fine)
beaten egg or milk

Mix the pork, basil or sage, egg, breadcrumbs, and salt and pepper together. The mixture should be very well seasoned. Roll out the pastry into an oblong about 20 by 25 cm/8 by 10 inches. Make the pork mixture into a long sausage shape and put it down the centre of the pastry. Roll the sides of the pastry over the mixture to form a large sausage roll. Brush the overlapping edges with water to stick them well together.

Turn the sausage roll on to a baking tray so that the join is underneath. Brush the surface with beaten egg or milk. Use pastry trimmings to decorate the pie, either with leaves or, simpler still, with a fine criss-cross lattice like Malvolio's legging thongs. Brush again with beaten egg and bake in a moderately hot oven (200°C, 400°F, Gas Mark 6) for 30 minutes to get the pastry good and brown, and then for a further 10 minutes with the oven turned down to moderate (160°C, 325°F, Gas Mark 3) to cook the sausage filling. Serve hot with salad.

SERVES FOUR TO FIVE

SIMPLE SAUSAGES WITH APPLE SAUCE

Of course good bought sausages can be used for this recipe but
they're becoming more and more difficult to find, most
of them tasting of nothing but preservative. And making your own
sausages is as easy as winking, especially if you
are prepared to dispense with the sausage casing. I find them
better without skins anyway.

METRIC/IMPERIAL
450 g/1 lb minced belly of pork
100 g/4 oz fresh white breadcrumbs
1 egg
½ teaspoon rubbed sage
salt and freshly ground black pepper
butter for frying
FOR THE SAUCE
50 g/2 oz butter
1 small onion, chopped
2 dessert apples, peeled and sliced
20 g/¾ oz flour
1 tablespoon sherry
150 ml/¼ pint chicken or veal stock
½ teaspoon French mustard
2 tablespoons double cream

To make the sausages, simply combine all the sausage ingredients
and season very well. Form into sausage shapes using floured hands
to stop the mixture sticking. Fry the sauasages in butter in a heavy
frying pan, turning them frequently to brown evenly all over. When
they are cooked remove them to a plate and keep warm.

In the same pan as you fried the sausages melt the butter and add
the onion. Cook slowly until the onion is soft and transparent, and
then add the sliced apples. Shake the pan over a moderate heat,
turning the apples carefully with a wooden spatula so as not to break
them, until they are soft and slightly brown. Sprinkle over the flour
and add the sherry, stock and mustard. Season well with salt and
pepper.

Stirring gently, bring the sauce to the boil. Allow it to simmer
gently for 10 minutes or so – just long enough to soften the harsh
taste of the sherry. If the sauce is now too thin, use a perforated
spoon to lift out the apple slices, putting them on top of the sausages.

Then boil the sauce rapidly to reduce it to a creamy consistency. Stir in the cream, reheat, and pour over the sausages.

SERVES FOUR

BOBOTIE

This is a South African dish, rather like a shepherd's pie, made with lamb and slightly curried. It reheats perfectly and is very successful as a party dish.

METRIC/IMPERIAL
1 large slice bread
300 ml/½ pint milk
1 small dessert apple
1 onion, finely chopped
25 g/1 oz butter
½ tablespoon curry powder
1 tablespoon mango chutney
1 tablespoon almonds
1 teaspoon seedless raisins
1 tablespoon lemon juice
450 g/1 lb minced cooked lamb
(half a shoulder of roast lamb would be perfect)
salt and pepper
FOR THE TOP
2 eggs
salt and pepper
few lemon leaves *or* lime leaves

Soak the bread in the milk. Set the oven to moderate (180°C, 350°F, Gas Mark 4) and grease a pie dish lightly.

Chop the apple and add with the chopped onion to the butter in a frying pan. Cook slowly until the apple is soft and the onion transparent. Stir in the curry powder and continue to cook for a further minute or so. Add the chutney, almonds, raisins, and lemon juice.

Squeeze the milk from the bread (but don't throw away the milk – you will need it later) and fork the bread into the meat. Tip the curry sauce with the meat and the forked bread into a bowl and mix well, seasoning with plenty of salt and pepper. Spread this mixture in the pie dish and put into the oven for 15 minutes.

Mix together the eggs and the milk in which the bread was soaked and season with salt and pepper. Once the meat has formed a slight crust or skin pour over the savoury custard and top with the lemon leaves. Return to the oven and bake for 35 minutes or until the top is slightly browned and the meat feels more solid than soft. Serve hot with rice.

SERVES FOUR

CASSOULET

METRIC/IMPERIAL
450 g/1 lb dried white haricot beans, soaked overnight
225 g/8 oz bacon *or* salt pork in 1 piece
1 onion, finely sliced
1 bay leaf
pinch of dried thyme
4 tablespoons bacon fat
450 g/1 lb breast of lamb
4 tomatoes, peeled
1 clove garlic, crushed
2 tablespoons tomato purée
salt and freshly ground black pepper
75 g/3 oz toasted breadcrumbs

Drain the beans and put them in a casserole with the bacon (perhaps cut into 2 or 3 largish chunks), the onion, herbs and 2 tablespoons of bacon fat. Cover with water and bring to the boil. Simmer for 30 minutes.

Cut the lamb into 2.5-cm/1-inch chunks. In a frying pan brown the chunks all over in the remaining bacon fat. Quarter the tomatoes and discard the seeds. Pack the lamb into the bottom of an ovenproof casserole and add the tomatoes. Then tip in the half-cooked beans and bacon, 300 ml/½ pint of the liquid from the cooking, and stir in the crushed garlic and the tomato purée. Taste and add salt and pepper if necessary. Sprinkle the top with the breadcrumbs and put on the lid.

Bake the cassoulet in a cool oven (150°C, 300°F, Gas Mark 2) for 2 hours. Then remove the lid to allow a crust to form. Return to the oven and continue to bake for a further 30 minutes or until the bacon and lamb are very tender and the beans soft. By this time the liquid should be absorbed.

SERVES FOUR

CHICKEN AND LIVER FRIKADELLE

METRIC/IMPERIAL
225 g/8 oz lamb's liver
225 g/8 oz cooked chicken
40 g/1½ oz butter
1 small onion, finely chopped
25 g/1 oz fresh white breadcrumbs
1 tablespoon cream
1 tablespoon beaten egg
salt and pepper
flour for dusting
butter for frying

Slice the liver thinly. Mince the cooked chicken. Melt the butter in a heavy frying pan and fry the liver slices until brown on both sides, but still pink in the middle. Lift out the liver and add the chopped onion to the pan. Turn down the heat to cook the onion slowly until it is soft and transparent.

Now mince together the contents of the frying pan and the cooked liver. Mix in the chicken, breadcrumbs, cream and beaten egg. Season well with salt and pepper,. Using floured hands, form the mixture into small flat patties and dust all over with flour. Just before serving fry these patties in butter until brown on both sides, and serve with tomato sauce (see page 45).

SERVES FOUR

PAPRIKA CHICKEN

METRIC/IMPERIAL
1 (1.5-kg/3½-lb) chicken
2 tablespoons oil
50 g/2 oz butter
2 tablespoons flour
salt and pepper
2 large mild onions, finely sliced
1 clove garlic, crushed
½ tablespoon paprika
2 tablespoons tomato purée
300 ml/½ pint white wine
300 ml/½ pint good chicken stock
1 tablespoon chopped parsley
pinch of rubbed thyme
1 (142-ml/5-fl oz) carton soured cream

Cut the chicken into 8 neat joints. In a heavy-bottomed saucepan heat the oil and add 25 g/1 oz of the butter. Roll the chicken pieces in the flour, well seasoned with salt and pepper. Shake off any excess flour and brown the chicken pieces in the foaming fat. As they brown lift them out and put into another saucepan or a casserole.

Now fry the sliced onions in the first pan, adding the rest of the butter if necessary. Cook the onions until they are soft and transparent and just beginning to turn colour. Add the crushed garlic and cook for a further half a minute. Stir in the paprika and the flour left over after coating the chicken joints. Stir in the tomato purée into the pan and mix until you have a smooth paste. Then pour in both the wine and the stock and stir until the mixture comes to the boil.

Pour this sauce over the chicken pieces and add the chopped parsley, thyme, and more salt and pepper if necessary. Barely simmer the contents of the pan until the chicken is tender. This should take 45–50 minutes.

Lift the chicken joints from the saucepan or casserole and put them on a warmed serving dish with a good lip. Spoon the sauce over the chicken joints and trickle the soured cream over the top.

SERVES FOUR

CHICKEN CURRY

METRIC/IMPERIAL
40 g/1½ oz flour
pinch of turmeric
pinch of cayenne
pinch of dried English mustard
pinch of crushed coriander
1 (1.5-kg/3-lb) chicken
2 tablespoons oil
2 medium onions, finely chopped
1 clove garlic, crushed
½ tablespoon curry powder *or* 1 teaspoon turmeric plus a pinch each
of cayenne, dried mustard and crushed coriander
300 ml/½ pint good chicken stock
1 bay leaf
½ tablespoon fresh chopped mint
½ tablespoon tomato purée
juice of 1 lemon
salt and pepper
1 tablespoon thick cream
1 tablespoon plain yogurt
1 tablespoon flaked almonds
TO SERVE
plain boiled rice

Mix the flour with the turmeric, cayenne, mustard and crushed coriander. Cut the chicken into 8 neat joints and roll each in the spiced flour. Heat the oil in a heavy-bottomed sauté pan or saucepan and fry the chicken joints all over until evenly brown. With a perforated spoon lift out the joints and put them in a roasting tin.

Now add the onions to the oil in the pan and fry until they are soft and just beginning to brown. Add the crushed garlic and the curry powder and cook for a further 2 minutes. Then add the stock, bay leaf, chopped mint, tomato purée and lemon juice. Stir well while bringing the sauce to the boil. Taste and add salt and pepper if necessary. Pour the sauce over the chicken joints in the roasting tin, cover the tin with foil and bake in a moderate oven (180°C, 350°F, Gas Mark 4) until the chicken is tender and cooked all the way through – about 50–60 minutes.

Lift the chicken joints on to the serving dish and add the cream, yogurt and almonds to the sauce in the roasting tin. Reheat without boiling and immediately pour over the chicken. Serve at once.

SERVES FOUR

SLIGHTLY CHINESE CHICKEN

METRIC/IMPERIAL
4 chicken breasts
cornflour
450 g/1 lb fresh French beans, topped and tailed
2 tablespoons oil
25 g/1 oz blanched almonds
lemon juice
3 tablespoons soy sauce
salt and freshly ground black pepper
TO SERVE
plain boiled rice

Cut the chicken breasts into small pieces and toss them in cornflour to lightly coat them. Immerse the French beans in boiling water and cook for 4 minutes. Drain them, then swish them under the cold tap to stop further cooking and set the colour.

Heat the oil in a large frying pan and toss the chicken breasts in it, turning them constantly with a fish slice, and shaking the pan so that they cook fairly fast and evenly. When they are almost cooked add the drained beans and continue frying until they are hot, and the chicken is cooked. With a perforated spoon lift both chicken and beans on to a warmed serving dish.

Put the blanched almonds into the frying pan and fry them fast, turning and stirring, until brown. Scatter them on top of the chicken and beans. Squeeze about 1 tablespoon lemon juice into the pan, add the soy sauce and heat briefly. Pour over the dish. Sprinkle lightly with salt, and grind black pepper over the top. Serve at once with plain boiled rice.

SERVES FOUR TO FIVE

CHICORY AND HAM MORNAY

METRIC/IMPERIAL
15 g/½ oz butter
2 tablespoons chopped onion
4 heads Belgian chicory (sometimes confusingly called endive)
150 ml/¼ pint chicken stock
salt and pepper
4 slices ham
FOR THE CHEESE SAUCE
20 g/¾ oz butter
20 g/¾ oz flour
300 ml/½ pint creamy milk
75 g/3 oz hard cheese, grated
pinch of cayenne
pinch of dried mustard
salt and freshly ground pepper
FOR THE TOP
25 g/1 oz Cheddar cheese, grated
1 tablespoon fresh white breadcrumbs

First set the oven to moderate (180°C, 350°F, Gas Mark 4). Use the first 15 g/½ oz of butter to grease a small ovenproof dish just large enough to hold the four heads of chicory. Add the chopped onion and the chicory, well washed. Add the stock and season with salt and pepper. Cover with foil or a lid and bake for 25 minutes or until the chicory is tender. Drain it well.

To make the sauce, melt the butter in a saucepan and stir in the flour. Cook for half a minute, stirring, then draw off the heat. Add the milk and, still stirring, return to the heat. Stir until the sauce boils then add the grated cheese and allow the cheese to melt. Once the cheese is added, do not boil the sauce. Season with cayenne, mustard, salt and pepper. If the sauce is very thick use some of the liquid in which the chicory was cooked to thin it slightly.

Wrap each piece of chicory in a slice of ham and pack tightly in a serving dish. Pour over the sauce and scatter the 25 g/1 oz of grated cheese and the breadcrumbs on top. Bake in the oven for 10 minutes to reheat the chicory, then transfer the dish to the grill to brown nicely.

SERVES FOUR

MUSHROOM FLORENTINE

METRIC/IMPERIAL
1.25 kg/2½ lb fresh spinach *or* 450 g/1 lb frozen spinach
50 g/2 oz butter
1 medium onion, finely chopped
175 g/6 oz dark flat mushrooms, sliced
6 tomatoes, sliced and peeled
6 hard-boiled eggs
600 ml/1 pint cheese sauce (see Chicory and
Ham Mornay), slightly warmed
grated cheese
dried white breadcrumbs
salt and freshly ground black pepper
grated nutmeg

Set the oven to moderately hot (200°C, 400°F, Gas Mark 6). Wash
the spinach and discard the tough stalks, put it into a heavy pan with
some salt but no water, and cook gently, covered, until tender.
Drain very well by pressing it between two plates. Chop roughly and
season to taste with salt, pepper and grated nutmeg.

Melt the butter, add the onion and cook it very slowly until soft
and transparent but not coloured. Add the sliced mushrooms and
cook for a further minute. Put the spinach on the bottom of a gratin
dish and spoon over the onion and mushroom mixture. Cover with
slices of tomato and hard-boiled eggs. Pour over the slightly warmed
cheese sauce and sprinkle liberally with grated cheese and dried
breadcrumbs. Heat in the oven for 15 minutes and put under a hot
grill until well browned.

SERVES SIX

VEGETARIAN STEW

*This is literally a stew made entirely of
vegetables substantial enough for a main course. The only
snag is it requires almost every vegetable in the
market, but is well worth the effort if one can manage
it. Variations are of course possible, the following
ingredients being only suggestions.*

METRIC/IMPERIAL
100 g/4 oz dried haricot beans, soaked for a few hours or overnight in water
50 g/2 oz butter
3 small onions, peeled
2 leeks, washed and cut into 2.5-cm/1-inch chunks
1 large or 2 small courgettes, cut into chunks
2 medium carrots, peeled and cut into sticks
2 sticks celery, sliced
3 small tomatoes, skinned
300 ml/½ pint vegetable stock
3 new potatoes, scrubbed but not peeled
salt and freshly ground black pepper
225 g/8 oz cauliflower, broken into sprigs
2 teaspoons flour
½ tablespoon chopped parsley
½ tablespoon chopped mint

Cook the soaked haricot beans in fresh boiling water until tender. This can take anything from 45 minutes–2 hours depending on the age and size of the beans. Drain them well. Put half the butter and the onions, leeks, courgettes, carrots, celery and tomatoes into a saucepan and cover tightly. Put over a moderate heat and cook slowly for 5 or 6 minutes.

Add the stock and bring up to the boil. Add the potatoes and salt and simmer for about 15 minutes. Then add the cauliflower and beans and continue to simmer until all the vegetables are tender – about another 15 minutes.

Make a paste of the remaining butter and the flour and slip this bit by bit into the pan, stirring all the time, to thicken the liquid for the vegetables. Simmer for 2 minutes, then add the parsley and the mint. Taste, adding more salt and pepper if necessary.

If this stew is to be served as a vegetarian main course, it might be a good idea to serve some boiled brown rice with it.

SERVES FOUR

VEGETARIAN CURRY

Follow the Vegetarian Stew recipe, omitting the haricot beans. In a second saucepan melt 25 g/1 oz butter and in it fry one large onion very finely sliced. Cook the onion until it is soft and just beginning to brown. Now stir in 1 teaspoon of very good curry paste, or curry powder, and cook for a further minute. Then add 1 tablespoon of sultanas, 1 teaspoon of apricot or plum jam and the juice of half a lemon. Stir this mixture into the vegetable stew and bring to the boil.

The vegetable curry is delicious served as it is, but improves if kept overnight and reheated the next day.

SERVES FOUR

VEGETABLE COUSCOUS

Couscous is made from wheat, and is rather like semolina, but coarser. In Middle Eastern countries it can mean anything from a sort of porridge to a luxury dish containing chicken, game, vegetables, etc.

METRIC/IMPERIAL
100 g/4 oz chick peas
100 g/4 oz couscous
450 ml/¾ pint chicken stock
4 button onions, peeled
2 leeks, washed and cut into chunks
1 carrot, peeled and cut into short sticks
1 stick celery, chopped into 2.5-cm/1-inch lengths
2 courgettes, cut in chunks
4 tomatoes, peeled
1 teaspoon chopped mint
1 tablespoon finely chopped parsley
pinch of dried oregano
pinch of saffron *or* a few shreds of saffron
soaked in 1 tablespoon water
FOR THE SAUCE
1 teaspoon ground cumin
1 teaspoon ground coriander
½ teaspoon chilli powder
2 tablespoons tomato purée
2 tablespoons hot stock taken from the cooking vegetables

Soak the chick peas in cold water overnight or until slightly swollen. Drain them and simmer in fresh water until tender – anything from 45 minutes–3 hours depending on the type and size of the chick peas. Put the couscous into a bowl and cover it with about 300 ml/½ pint of cold water. Leave to absorb liquid for 10 minutes.

Ideally, to cook the couscous you should have a double steamer, or a special *couscousier*, but a wire sieve lined with a muslin cloth will do. Bring the chicken stock to the boil in the bottom of the steamer and add the onions, leeks, carrot and celery. Put the softened couscous into the lined sieve or top half of the steamer and set it over the boiling vegetables. Cover tightly. (This might involve using foil as well as the saucepan lid if you are using the sieve-and-muslin method. The idea is to prevent steam escaping so that the couscous will cook in the vegetable steam.)

Simmer for 30 minutes and then add the courgettes to the vegetables under the couscous. Fork the couscous to remove any lumps and return the lid (and foil if necessary). Cook for a further 10 minutes, then add the tomatoes, mint, parsley and oregano to the vegetable mixture and cook for another 10 minutes. Tip the couscous into a serving dish and keep warm. Drain off some of the stock – the vegetables should be wet but not swimming in liquid. Add the saffron (with its water if necessary) to the vegetables and stir in the chick peas.

Use 2 tablespoons of the drained-off stock to moisten the cumin, coriander, chilli powder and tomato purée. This makes a small amount of very hot spicy sauce. Put it into a sauce or gravy boat. To serve the couscous spread it flat on a serving dish and pile the vegetables on top of it. Hand the sauce separately.

SERVES' FOUR

LUCULLUS EGGS

METRIC/IMPERIAL
50 g/2 oz butter
1 medium lettuce, chopped
225 g/8 oz mushrooms, sliced
salt and pepper
4 eggs
2 tablespoons thick cream
40 g/1½ oz Cheddar cheese, grated

Butter a shallow ovenproof dish lightly. Set the oven to moderate (180°C, 350°F, Gas Mark 4). Melt half the butter in a saucepan and add the chopped lettuce and sliced mushrooms, seasoning well with salt and pepper. Put the lid on the pan and shake over the heat until the mushrooms are slightly softened, and the lettuce cooked.

With a perforated spoon lift the lettuce and mushrooms from the pan (leaving behind the juices) and put into the buttered dish. Fork in the rest of the butter and then make four dips in the mixture using the back of a large spoon. Into these dips carefully break the four eggs. Spoon the cream over the top of each egg and sprinkle the whole dish with the grated cheese.

Put into the preheated oven for 10–12 minutes or until the egg white is set, the yolks still runny, and the cheese just melted.

SERVES FOUR

PORTUGUESE EGGS

METRIC/IMPERIAL
4 hard-boiled eggs
75 g/3 oz butter
salt and freshly ground black pepper
1 clove garlic, crushed
4 large ripe tomatoes
1 tablespoon chopped parsley
50 g/2 oz strong Cheddar cheese, grated
1 tablespoon dried breadcrumbs
FOR THE SAUCE
40 g/¾ oz butter
40 g/¾ oz flour
300 ml/½ pint creamy milk
1 bay leaf
slice of onion
salt and pepper

First make the sauce: melt the butter in a saucepan and stir in the flour. Cook for half a minute, stirring. Add the milk and stir continuously while bringing to the boil. Add the bay leaf and the slice of onion, and salt and pepper to taste. Leave the sauce to infuse while you get on with the eggs.

Set the oven to moderately hot (200°C, 400°F, Gas Mark 6) and heat the grill. With a stainless steel knife, slice the eggs roughly. Use half the butter to generously butter a pie dish. Into this put the sliced eggs, with plenty of salt and pepper. Melt the rest of the butter in a frying pan and in it cook the crushed garlic for half a minute.

Dunk the tomatoes in boiling water for 5 seconds, and peel them. Slice roughly and then fry fairly quickly in the garlicky butter until just beginning to soften. They should not break up at all. Scatter the parsley over the eggs and then cover with the tomatoes.

Remove the onion and bay leaf from the sauce, and pour evenly over the tomatoes in the pie dish. Mix the grated cheese and the breadcrumbs together and evenly cover the top of the dish. Heat through in the oven for about 10 minutes and then place under the grill to brown on top. Serve immediately, while the top is still bubbling.

SERVES FOUR

PIZZA

*Pizza is essentially a bread base baked with some
savoury topping, generally containing tomatoes and cheese
although many variations are possible – see suggestions below.
This basic pizza dough serves 2 people as a main course or 4
people as a starter, or perhaps more as a picnic or cocktail snack.*

METRIC/IMPERIAL
150 ml/¼ pint lukewarm milk *or*
150 ml/¼ pint half milk and half water
15 g/½ oz fresh yeast
2 teaspoons castor sugar
225 g/8 oz plain flour
½ teaspoon salt
1–1½ tablespoons olive oil

Warm the liquid and mix a tablespoon or so of it with the yeast and
the sugar. Cream this mixture with a teaspoon and then add it to the
rest of the liquid. Sift the flour with the salt into a large warm bowl
and make a hollow in the centre. Pour the yeasty liquid into this
hollow and, stirring with a knife, mix well. Using a floured hand
form the mixture into a soft dough. Turn on to a floured board or
table top and knead energetically for 10 minutes or so until you have
an elastic, not sticky, dough.

Roll and push the dough into a plate-sized flat shape and with your
fingertips make deep dimples all over it. Trickle a little bit of the
olive oil into each one of these dips, and then fold the dough over to
enclose the oil. Knead once more until again shiny and elastic. Make
the dough into a ball and rub a thin film of oil all over it. Put the ball
of dough back into the bowl, stretch a piece of polythene across the
top of the bowl and put it in a warm place until it has doubled in size.
This should take anything from 45 minutes–2 hours, depending on
the warmth.

Place the dough on a floured surface. Divide the ball into 2 pieces
and roll each out into a large thin round, preferably about 25–30
cm/10–12 inches across. Alternatively make 4 pizzas about the size
of a dessert plate and put them into sandwich tins to cook. If you are
making the large ones they will need to go on flat baking trays. Draw
the edges up slightly with the fingers to make a rim to the pizza to
prevent sloppy fillings from spilling. Cover the pizza with the chosen
filling ingredients, and leave for 10 minutes or so before baking.

In the meantime preheat the oven to 200°C, 425°F, Gas Mark 7.

Bake the pizza for 15–20 minutes or until the edges are puffy and risen and slightly brown, and the bread base underneath is cooked (to test slide a large fish slice underneath the pizza, lift it up and have a look). Serve the pizza as quickly as possible after baking as they toughen considerably as they cool, and are not nearly as good.

PIZZA TOPPINGS
Cream Cheese and Anchovy

METRIC/IMPERIAL
100 g/4 oz cream cheese, cut into dice
1 (56-g/2-oz) can anchovy fillets, drained and split lengthwise
small handful of black olives, stoned
1 teaspoon chopped fresh marjoram *or*
½ teaspoon dried oregano
2 tablespoons grated Cheddar cheese
olive oil

When the dough is ready for the topping simply scatter the cream cheese evenly all over, lattice with the anchovy fillets, and scatter the olives, oregano and Cheddar evenly all over the top. Sprinkle with oil.

Tomato and Salami

METRIC/IMPERIAL
olive oil
2 cloves garlic, crushed
1 tablespoon finely chopped fresh basil
1 Spanish onion, finely chopped
salt and plenty of black pepper
8 tomatoes, peeled and finely sliced
75 g/3 oz salami, skinned and sliced as finely as possible

First mix the oil, garlic and chopped basil together and spread this evenly over the dough, avoiding the very edge. Then scatter the chopped onion over, and season well with salt and pepper. Arrange the slices of tomato and salami on top.

SERVES TWO OR FOUR

LASAGNE RING MOULD

METRIC/IMPERIAL
225 g/8 oz lasagne or cannelloni pasta
2 rashers streaky bacon, with rind removed, chopped
1 medium onion, finely chopped
50 g/2 oz Cheddar cheese, grated
1 whole egg and 1 egg yolk
150 ml/¼ pint cream
150 ml/¼ pint milk
salt and freshly ground black pepper
1 tablespoon butter
squeeze of lemon juice
1 tablespoon chopped chervil or chopped parsley

Cook the lasagne or cannelloni according to the instructions on the packet. Drain it well under running hot water to rinse off any starch. Butter a ring mould or bread tin and line it with the cooked pasta, overlapping the pieces slightly.

To make the filling, put the chopped bacon into a heavy frying pan and cook gently until the bacon is just beginning to brown. Add the chopped onion and cook it in the bacon fat. If the pan becomes too dry you may need to add a teaspoon of butter. When the onion is transparent and soft, remove the pan from the heat.

In a bowl mix together the grated cheese, eggs, cream and milk. Now add the contents from the frying pan and taste for seasoning, adding salt and pepper if necessary. Tip this mixture carefully into the pasta-lined ring mould or bread tin, stand the tin in a roasting tin two thirds full of hot water and bake in a moderately hot oven (190°C, 375°F, Gas Mark 5) for 25 minutes or so until the custard mixture is set and just beginning to brown. Turn the mould out on to a heated serving dish. To do this put the serving dish over the mould and, using a thick cloth to protect your hands from the heat, turn the mould and plate over together and give a sharp shake.

In a pan heat together the butter, lemon juice and the chopped chervil or parsley. Pour this over the mould just before serving.

SERVES FOUR

EASY PARTY PASTA

METRIC/IMPERIAL
450 g/1 lb pasta shells *or* macaroni pieces, tagliatelle, etc.
2 medium onions, finely sliced
oil or butter for frying
225 g/8 oz mushrooms, sliced
1 clove garlic, crushed
4 large tomatoes, peeled and quartered
4 slices ham, cut into thin strips
75 g/3 oz Cheddar cheese, grated
chives or spring onion tops, chopped

Cook the pasta according to the instructions on the packet, drain well and rinse off any excess starch in running hot water. Toss the cooked pasta in just enough oil or butter to stop it sticking together.

In heavy frying pan gently cook the sliced onions in butter or oil until they are soft and transparent, then add the mushrooms and continue cooking for a further minute or two. Add the crushed garlic and finally the peeled tomatoes and the strips of ham. Shake the pan over the heat until everything is hot but not browned. With a fork mix the contents of the pan into the hot pasta and fork in the grated cheese and the chives. Turn into a hot dish and serve immediately, preferably with a green salad.

If this dish is to be made in advance, the onion, mushroom and ham mixture can be reheated successfully. The pasta can be pre-cooked and simply dunked into boiling water to reheat. Alternatively it can be buttered and reheated in the oven. The cheese and chives must go in at the last minute, however.

SERVES FOUR TO FIVE

HOME-MADE PASTA

*Making your own pasta is very satisfying and pleasurable.
It is not difficult but you need plenty of table top,
and a not-too-busy morning.*

METRIC/IMPERIAL
450 g/1 lb plain flour (preferably strong flour *or* semolina flour)
4 large eggs
good pinch of salt
1 tablespoon oil

Sift the flour on to the table top. Make a well in the middle and into it break the eggs and add the salt and oil. With the fingers of one hand work the eggs together, gradually bringing in the flour and kneading to a stiff paste. You may need to add a tablespoon or two of warm water to get an adhesive dough. If it sticks to your hand, use a knife in your clean hand to scrape it off. Using as little flour as you can to prevent sticking, knead and work the dough for 10–15 minutes or until it is smooth and elastic. Wrap the dough in polythene or a damp cloth and leave for 30 minutes.

Roll out, paper-thin, over the whole table top – the quantity should stretch to a sheet about twice the size of a pillowcase. If it hangs over the table top, no matter, just keep rolling sections of it at a time until it is really thin. Alternatively, cut the dough into four, and work with one small bit at a time. Then cut it into ribbons, squares, triangles or strips. Hang these over a laundry rail or back of a chair, or stretch them out on a cake rack, or spread them on a tea towel to dry for an hour before cooking.

Bringing a large pan of salted water to the boil, and when bubbling, drop in the pasta. Cooking time depends on the thickness of the noodles. It can be as little as 3 minutes, as much as 20. Five or 6 minutes is usual for thin tagliatelli if cooking fresh pasta. If it is dried, double the cooking times. It is cooked when soft enough to chew easily, but still with a bit of bite (*al dente*). Test occasionally by extracting a piece from the boiling water and biting it.

When done, drain the pasta, wash it well with plenty of hot or boiling water (this is to get rid of excess starch which makes it stick stodgily together), then toss in oil, butter, or sauce. Serve as soon as reasonably possible.

PASTA AL PESTO

*This recipe is essentially noodles with garlic and
basil, but the addition of Parmesan cheese and pine nuts
makes it rich and substantial enough for a main course. I
think it is my favourite food in all the world.*

*Italians argue about the authenticity of a recipe with
Parmesan instead of Pecorino, or whether it should be made
with or without the pine nuts (or walnuts which are sometimes
used), but such esoteric nonsense is not for us. Just
make the pesto, and enjoy it. It keeps for a month in a
larder, two months in a fridge, and you need about a
tablespoon per portion of pasta.*

METRIC/IMPERIAL
3 cloves garlic
2 large cups (1 large bunch) basil leaves
75 g/3 oz Pecorino or Parmesan cheese, finely grated
olive oil
50 g/2 oz pine nuts
salt and pepper

In a liquidiser or mortar, grind the garlic and basil together to a
paste. Add the cheese, and enough olive oil to double the quantity
you have. Add the whole pine nuts, and salt and pepper to taste. As
soon as the pasta is cooked, rinsed and drained, add a tablespoon of
pesto for each guest to be served, and mix well.

Puddings

YOGURT

Yogurt is easy to make at home and much cheaper than when bought in a shop. It is best made with long-life sterilised milk, or with skimmed milk for a low-fat yogurt. It can be made entirely or partly from cream, or with extra milk powder added to the milk to give a wonderfully rich luxurious yogurt. Yogurt made from pasteurised milk must be thoroughly boiled first, and allowed to cool to lukewarm before use. The boiling is to destroy unwanted bacteria in the milk which could interfere with the bacterial action of the yogurt culture. Sterilised milk (either bottled with a crown cork, or evaporated tinned milk, reconstituted) works very reliably.

METRIC/IMPERIAL
600 ml/1 pint milk (boiled or sterilised)
1 tablespoon natural yogurt, well within date code

Warm the milk until lukewarm (or cool it to lukewarm if it has been boiled). Stir in the yogurt. Pour into a bowl or dish and put into a warm draught-free place until set. This usually takes about 14 hours. The cooler the temperature, the slower the yogurt will take, but too great a temperature will kill the culture and the yogurt will not form.

Yogurt can be set in a warm airing cupboard or boiler room, a very cool electric oven (set as low as possible), a vacuum flask with a wide neck, or an insulated ice-bucket. Or it can be made in a bowl set in a larger bowl of warm water, standing in the sink with the hot tap dripping steadily into the outer bowl to keep the water warm. An earthenware pot with a lid, wrapped up in a warm blanket and put near a radiator, will do the job too.

The simple aim is to provide steady, even warmth to allow the culture to develop.

GREEK YOGURT

*This is so simple I am almost ashamed to include it in
a sophisticated cookbook. But it is so good I'd be more ashamed
to omit it. Best with home-made yogurt, but still good
with the commercial kind.*

METRIC/IMPERIAL
plain yogurt
fresh cream
Jordan almonds, unskinned
fresh or soft dried dates, quartered
runny honey

Spoon the yogurt into serving dishes. Chill well. Just before serving
cover the top liberally with cream (not whipped, just as it is), then
scatter over it almonds and dates.

Trickle a little honey all over everything and serve at once.

A CHEAT'S CRÈME BRÛLÉE

*This is a version of the famous Trinity College crème
brûlée, but without the anxiety of grilling the
caramel top. In this version the caramel is simply poured
over the set custard.*

METRIC/IMPERIAL
300 ml/½ pint double cream
3 drops vanilla essence
4 egg yolks
50 g/2 oz castor sugar
FOR THE TOPPING
75 g/3 oz granulated sugar

Start the day before you plan to eat the crème brûlée. Put the cream
and vanilla essence into a pan and heat up to scalding point (when
the cream is just beginning to bubble round the edges). Beat the egg
yolks and the castor sugar until light and fluffy. Pour on the hot
cream, stirring until the sugar has dissolved.

Set the oven to moderate (160°C, 325°F, Gas Mark 3). Strain the
custard into a shallow pie dish, or into individual ramekin dishes.
Stand the custard, or custards, in a roasting tin half-filled with hot

water and put into the oven to bake. The small custards will probably require about 12 minutes, the large one about 30 minutes. The custard should be not quite set, but should have a good skin on top of it. Resist the temptation to touch the skin – it breaks very easily. Refrigerate the custard overnight.

The next day, about an hour or so before your meal, put the castor sugar into a heavy-bottomed saucepan and set it over a gentle heat. Allow it first to melt, then turn the heat up so that the sugar will brown to an even brown, runny toffee. As soon as you reach this stage, stand the caramel pan in a bowl of cold water – it will sizzle alarmingly you do this, but never fear: this is to cool the caramel rapidly. As soon as the toffee has stopped bubbling carefully pour it, or spoon it, in an even sheet all over the set custard top. Allow the toffee to cool and become crackly.

To serve, crack the top with the serving spoon and give each diner some of the custard, and a piece of hard toffee.

NOTE To remove the caramel from the saucepan or the spoons, cover them with water and boil. The toffee will melt and be easy to wash off.

SERVES FOUR ·

ORANGE JELLY WITH CARAMEL CHIPS

METRIC/IMPERIAL
FOR THE ORANGE JELLY
600 ml/1 pint orange juice, fresh, canned or frozen (but not diluted orange squash)
65 g/2½ oz granulated sugar
20 g/¾ oz powdered gelatine
FOR THE TOPPING
50 g/2 oz granulated sugar
300 ml/½ pint double cream

Warm the orange juice slightly, but on no account bring it to the boil (boiling changes the flavour). Put the sugar and gelatine into a small heavy-bottomed saucepan and pour on 4½ tablespoons water. Leave to 'sponge' for 10 minutes, then dissolve over a gentle heat, without allowing the gelatine to boil and resisting the temptation to stir it. When it is clear and liquid mix with the orange juice and pour into a wet plain jelly mould or pudding basin. Chill for at least 3 hours (preferably overnight) to set.

To make the caramel topping: put the granulated sugar into a small heavy saucepan and heat very slowly until the sugar first melts and then turns into a clear brown toffee. While the sugar is melting, lightly oil a baking tray. When you have a clear brown caramel pour it immediately on to the baking tray and leave to cool and harden. Once it is quite cold and brittle, break it into fine chips or slivers with the end of a rolling pin and put immediately into an airtight container until needed (caramel left in the atmosphere will become sticky).

Put a serving plate over the top of the jelly mould and turn the jelly and plate over together, giving a sharp shake to dislodge the jelly. If the jelly won't budge, dip the mould briefly into hot water to loosen the sides.

Whip the cream until it is just stiff enough to hold its shape and use it to mask the jelly completely. Just before serving scatter the caramel chips over the jelly.

SERVES FOUR

APRICOT AND PRUNE JELLY

METRIC/IMPERIAL
50 g/2 oz prunes
50 g/2 oz dried apricots
about 2 tablespoons sugar
pinch of cinnamon
300 ml/½ pint fresh, frozen or canned orange juice
1 tablespoon powdered gelatine

Put the prunes and apricots in a saucepan and cover with water. Let them soak for 2–3 hours and then simmer them gently until the prunes are soft enough for you to remove the stones and the apricots are tender. Keep the liquid that you cooked them in.

Put this liquid back into the saucepan and add sugar to taste and cinnamon. Stir until the sugar has dissolved. Measure the amount of this liquid you have, and if necessary make up to 300 ml/½ pint. Add it to the orange juice.

In the saucepan put 3 tablespoons of water (or 3 more tablespoons of the prune liquid if you have any left) and on to it sprinkle the gelatine. Leave to 'sponge' for 10 minutes and then heat very gently until the gelatine has dissolved and is clear and runny. Stir it into the orange juice and prune liquid.

Put the stoned prunes and the cooked apricots into the base of a 1.25-ml/2-pint pudding basin. Pour the orange mixture on top and leave to set, preferably overnight in the fridge.

To turn the jelly out, dip the pudding basin into hot water briefly. Loosen the edges of the jelly with your fingertips. Put a plate over the top of the basin and turn plate and jelly over together, giving a sharp shake to dislodge the jelly. Serve with real egg custard (see page 79).

SERVES FOUR

APRICOT AND ORANGE FOOL

METRIC/IMPERIAL
2 oranges
225 g/8 oz dried apricots, soaked overnight
about 3 tablespoons castor sugar
200 ml/7 fl oz double cream

Using a potato peeler, carefully pare all the rinds from the oranges, making sure that only the zest or outer skin is taken. Squeeze the juice from the oranges. Put the orange juice and rind, apricots and their water, and sugar together in a saucepan with a lid and simmer very slowly until the apricots are soft. If there is more than half a cup of liquid at the end of the cooking time, turn the heat up and boil rapidly until reduced to about half a cup. Liquidise or sieve the apricots and the orange rind, with the remaining juice. Allow to cool completely.

Whip the cream until it is stiff enough to just hold its shape. Stir the apricot mixture into the cream, swirling it to give a striped effect, and put into small pots or glasses. Chill well before serving.

SERVES FOUR

FRIED SYRUP DUMPLINGS

METRIC/IMPERIAL
50 g/2 oz butter
75 g/3 oz self-raising flour
50 g/2 oz fresh white breadcrumbs
good pinch of salt
1 egg
FOR THE SYRUP
450 ml/¾ pint water
175 g/6 oz granulated sugar
2 tablespoons golden syrup

First make the syrup: put the water, sugar and golden syrup together in a saucepan and heat slowly until the sugar has dissolved and the syrup feels tacky. Keep hot.

Rub the butter into the flour. Add the breadcrumbs and the salt. With a knife stir the egg into the mixture to bind it to a soft dough. Roll the dough into small balls between the palms of your hands.

Heat fat in a deep fryer until a crumb will sizzle vigorously in it, then deep-fry the balls until brown and crisp. Put them in a serving dish. Just before serving pour over the hot sauce.

The dumplings may be baked in a moderate oven, like cookies, if preferred.

SERVES FOUR

EASY ORANGE SORBET

METRIC/IMPERIAL
2 heaped tablespoons granulated sugar
300 ml/½ pint water
1 heaped teaspoon powdered gelatine
1 (177-g/6¼-oz) carton frozen
concentrated orange juice
2 egg whites

Put the sugar into a small saucepan and pour on the water. Sprinkle over the gelatine and set aside to soak, without stirring, for 10 minutes. Then warm gently until the gelatine and the sugar dissolve and you have a clear syrup. Allow to cool. Run the hot tap over the concentrated orange juice carton to release the block of frozen juice and tip it into a large bowl. Mix with the warm syrup, stirring well until quite smooth. When stone cold pour into freezing trays and freeze for about 1½ hours or until frozen round the edges and still sloppy in the middle.

In a large bowl whisk the egg whites until stiff but not dry looking. Tip the orange mixture on to the egg whites and mix together. Return the mixture to the freezing trays and freeze for a further hour. While the sorbet is freezing put a bowl and a whisk into the refrigerator to chill.

After an hour take the sorbet out of the freezer again, tip it into the chilled bowl and once again whisk until smooth. Return once more to the freezing trays and this time freeze until solid.

SERVES FOUR TO FIVE

RHUBARB OR GOOSEBERRY CAKE

METRIC/IMPERIAL
FOR THE CAKE
100 g/4 oz butter
100 g/4 oz sugar
2 eggs
100 g/4 oz self-raising flour, sifted
with a pinch of salt
little milk
FOR THE FILLING
225 g/8 oz rhubarb, cut into 2.5-cm/1-inch pieces, *or* 225 g/8 oz
topped and tailed fresh ripe gooseberries
1 tablespoon sugar
FOR THE TOPPING
50 g/2 oz butter
75 g/3 oz plain flour
25 g/1 oz sugar

Prepare a 20-cm/8-inch deep round cake tin or small roasting tin: brush it with melted butter or oil, dust with flour and then line with greaseproof paper. Repeat the greasing and flouring procedure.

Set the oven to moderately hot (190°C, 375°F, Gas Mark 5). While it is heating make the crumble topping by simply rubbing the butter into the flour and adding the sugar. Put into the refrigerator while you make the cake.

Cream the butter with the sugar until the mixture is very pale, light and soft. Lightly beat the eggs and add them to the sugar/

butter mixture, beating in a little at a time and folding a tablespoon or so of flour into the mixture at the same time – a spoon of egg followed by a spoon of flour and so on. If the mixture becomes too stiff (it should fall off the spoon rather reluctantly), stir in a few tablespoons of milk. Turn the cake mixture into the prepared tin and put the rhubarb pieces or gooseberries over the surface of the mixture, sprinkle with sugar and spread them as evenly as possible. Sprinkle the crumble mixture on the top and bake in the middle of the oven for 45–55 minutes or until the cake feels firm to the touch. Leave to cool in the tin.

NOTE This cake is moist and fairly hefty. Delicious as a tea-time snack, or as picnic food. Or for pudding, served with creamy custard. It is best eaten while the crumble topping is still crunchy – after a day or two in a tin it becomes soft.   SERVES FOUR TO SIX

APRICOT AND PRUNE UPSIDE-DOWN CAKE

METRIC/IMPERIAL
175 g/6 oz dried apricots
175 g/6 oz dried prunes
40 g/1½ oz butter
40 g/1½ oz brown sugar
FOR THE PUDDING MIXTURE
100 g/4 oz butter
100 g/4 oz castor sugar
2 large eggs
175 g/6 oz self-raising flour
milk

Put the apricots and prunes into a saucepan, cover with water and leave to soak for a few hours, then simmer gently until the apricots are soft and the stones will come out of the prunes easily. Chop the prunes and apricots roughly.

Set the oven to moderately hot (190°C, 375°F, Gas Mark 5). Butter the bottom of a 20-cm/8-inch square cake tin with most of the 40 g/1½ oz butter and then butter the sides of the tin more sparingly. Flour the sides of the tin and sprinkle the brown sugar over the bottom as evenly as you can. Arrange the roughly chopped dried fruit on the butter/sugar base.

To make the pudding mixture: cream the butter and sugar until light in colour and soft. Beat the eggs lightly and add them to the mixture gradually, beating as you go. Sift the flour into the mixture and fold in with a large metal spoon. Add enough milk to produce a soft dropping consistency (that is, it should fall off a spoon in blobs, but reluctantly). Spread the mixture on top of the fruit in the tin and bake for 45–50 minutes or until firm to the touch. If the pudding appears to be browning too fast either cover it well with wet greaseproof paper and foil, or reduce the heat in the oven to cool (150°C, 300°F, Gas Mark 2).

Turn the pudding out and serve hot with custard. Or allow it to cool in the tin and turn out to serve as a cake for tea.

SERVES FOUR TO SIX

REAL EGG CUSTARD

Making an egg custard (as opposed to one produced from a packet or a tin) can be a performance, carrying with it the awful risk of scrambling the eggs. This is a slight cheat, but the result is indistinguishable from the real thing and is much easier to manage.

METRIC/IMPERIAL
½ tablespoon cornflour *or* custard powder
600 ml/1 pint creamy milk
4 egg yolks
1 tablespoon castor sugar
2 drops vanilla essence

In a teacup blend the custard powder or cornflour with a little of the milk. Heat the rest of the milk, and when boiling pour some of it on to the blended cornflour or custard in the cup. Stir well and pour this mixture back into the hot milk, stirring until you have an evenly, slightly thickened sauce. Allow to simmer for 2–3 minutes.

In a bowl beat together the 4 egg yolks and castor sugar. Take the milk off the heat, allow it to stop bubbling and to cool for a few seconds, then pour it from a slight height on to the egg yolk and sugar mixture, stirring thoroughly as you do so. The heat will slightly cook the egg yolks, making the custard thicker. Add the vanilla essence and pour into a sauceboat or serving dish.

If in spite of all your precautions you have slightly scrambled the eggs, simply sieve the custard. It will taste fine but won't be quite as thick as intended.   SERVES FOUR

SEMOLINA CREAM WITH BLACKCURRANT SAUCE

METRIC/IMPERIAL
600 ml/1 pint milk
100 g/4 oz semolina
2 eggs
75 g/3 oz castor sugar
juice of 1 lemon
2 drops vanilla essence
4 tablespoons double cream
FOR THE SAUCE
450 g/1 lb fresh or frozen blackcurrants
water
about 100 g/4 oz sugar

Lightly butter a 1.5-litre/2½-pint pudding basin, heat the milk and stir in the semolina. Simmer, stirring occasionally, for 5–10 minutes or until the semolina is cooked. Remove from the heat and allow to cool slightly.

Separate the eggs and whisk the yolks and sugar until light and very fluffy. Then stir into the semolina mixture. Add the lemon juice, vanilla essence and the cream. Now whisk the egg whites and using a large metal spoon fold them into the mixture. Turn into the pudding basin and leave in the refrigerator to set.

To make the sauce: put the blackcurrants in a saucepan, add a cupful of water and cook until soft and mushy. Strain both juice and fruit through a sieve to extract the seeds and any stalks. Sweeten with sugar while the sauce is still hot enough to dissolve the sugar and set aside.

When ready to serve the pudding, run a knife round the edge of the semolina mould and turn it out on to a serving plate. Pour over the blackcurrant sauce and serve immediately.

SERVES FOUR

BREAD AND BUTTER PUDDING

Memories of school dinners have jaundiced our attitude to this pudding, but properly made it can be an absolute delight.

METRIC/IMPERIAL
3 large slices of plain white bread, with the crusts off
25 g/1 oz butter
1 tablespoon currants
1 tablespoon sultanas
about 1 tablespoon sugar
2 whole eggs and 1 egg yolk
450 ml/¾ pint creamy milk
few drops vanilla essence

Spread the bread slices liberally with butter. Butter a fairly shallow ovenproof dish. Cut the bread across into triangles and lay these triangles, only slightly overlapping, in the dish, butter side up. Sprinkle with the currants and sultanas and a teaspoon or so of sugar. Mix the eggs with the extra yolk, the milk and the vanilla essence. Taste and add enough sugar to make it barely sweet. Strain the custard over the bread and leave to soak for 30 minutes or so.

Heat the oven to moderate (180°C, 350°F, Gas Mark 4). Stand the dish in a roasting tin filled with 1 cm/½ inch or so of hot water. Put the pudding, water bath and all, into the oven and bake for 45 minutes.

On serving, the custard should be set, the top brown and crusty, and the whole pudding slightly puffy.

SERVES FOUR

CREAMY RICE PUDDING WTH RHUBARB SAUCE

METRIC/IMPERIAL
about 1 tablespoon butter
75 g/3 oz round-grain rice
900 ml/1½ pints creamy milk
1 tablespoon sugar
few drops vanilla essence
FOR THE SAUCE
225 g/½ lb fresh or frozen rhubarb
6 tablespoons water
sugar to taste

Butter the pie dish liberally, scatter the rice in the bottom of it, pour in the milk and add the sugar and vanilla essence. Bake in a cool oven (about 150°C, 300°F, Gas Mark 2) for 4 hours or so or until the rice has absorbed the milk, a good brown skin has formed, but the pudding is not yet stodgy or dry. It is a good idea to give the whole thing a thorough stir after about an hour of cooking.

To make the sauce: simply stew the rhubarb in water, adding enough sugar to give a sweet but still tart sauce, and blend to a smooth purée in the liquidiser. If the rice pudding is to be served hot serve the sauce chilled, and vice versa.

SERVES FOUR

TREACLE TART

METRIC/IMPERIAL
FOR THE PASTRY
225 g/8 oz plain flour
pinch of salt
150 g/5 oz butter
½ tablespoon castor sugar
1 egg yolk
squeeze of lemon juice
3 tablespoons icy water
FOR THE FILLING
about 8 tablespoons golden syrup
grated rind of ½ lemon
2 teaspoons lemon juice
about 3 heaped tablespoons
fresh white breadcrumbs

Sift the flour with the salt and rub in the butter until the mixture looks like coarse breadcrumbs. With a fork add the sugar and the egg yolk, mixed with the lemon juice and half the cold water. Mix to a firm dough, using first the fork and then your hand. Don't add the rest of the water unless the pastry is dry and crumbly.

Roll the pastry out and use it to line a 20-cm/8-inch flan ring. Prick the bottom all over with a fork and half fill the pastry case with an even layer of breadcrumbs. Mix the lemon rind and the 2 teaspoons of lemon juice into the golden syrup and pour that carefully over the crumbs, resisting the temptation to 'help' with the fork – you will only stir the crumbs up and spoil the appearance of the dish. (If the syrup has come out of a very cold larder and is not good and runny, warm it gently before pouring over the crumbs.)

Bake in a moderately hot oven (190°C, 375°F, Gas Mark 5) for about 30 minutes – or until the filling is not quite set, but perceptibly thickened, and the pastry is brown. If the tart is to be eaten cold it doesn't matter if the filling is almost runny when it comes out of the oven, because it will harden as it cools.

SERVES FOUR TO SIX

QUEEN'S PUDDING

METRIC/IMPERIAL
300 ml/½ pint milk
15 g/½ oz butter
150 g/5 oz castor sugar
2 tablespoons fresh white breadcrumbs
finely grated rind of 1 large lemon
2 eggs
2 tablespoons jam, preferably raspberry

Butter a pie dish. Heat the milk with the 15 g/½ oz of butter and 25 g/1 oz of the sugar, stirring until the sugar dissolves. Take off the heat and stir in the breadcrumbs and the finely grated lemon rind. Allow the mixture to cool slightly, then separate the eggs and beat the yolks into the mixture. Pour this custard into the pie dish and leave to stand for 1 hour or so.

Bake the pudding in a moderately hot oven (190°C, 375°F, Gas Mark 5) for 25 minutes or until the custard mixture is just solid. Take out of the oven and set aside to cool slightly.

Warm the jam until it is almost runny and easy to spread and pour it or spread it evenly over the top of the custard. Whisk the egg whites until stiff and into them beat half the remaining sugar. Whisk again until the meringue mixture is stiff and shiny and then fold in the rest of the sugar. Carefully spoon the meringue mixture on top of the custard, covering it completely. Dust with a fine layer of castor sugar. Put the pudding back into the oven until the meringue is just set and straw-coloured – this will take 10–15 minutes. Serve hot with thick cream.

SERVES FOUR

APPLES BAKED IN HONEY AND CIDER

METRIC/IMPERIAL
4 large cooking apples
25 g/1 oz butter, melted
3 tablespoons dried white breadcrumbs
1 tablespoon sultanas
finely grated rind and juice of 1 orange
2 tablespoons honey

Core the apples and peel the top half of each one only. Brush the apples all over with melted butter and roll them in the dried breadcrumbs. Butter a pie dish and stand the apples, skinned side up, in it. Fill the centre hole of each apple with the sultanas, mixed with the grated orange rind. Spoon about a teaspoon of honey over each apple, and add the cider and orange juice to the dish.

Bake the apples in a moderately hot oven (190°C, 375°F, Gas Mark 5) until they are soft right through, and brown on top. The juice should be spooned over the apples every 10 minutes or so. Cooking time will probably be about 40 minutes. Serve hot with thick cream.

SERVES FOUR

GINGER AND CHOCOLATE PROFITEROLES

METRIC/IMPERIAL
FOR THE PROFITEROLES
75 g/3 oz butter
225 ml/7½ fl oz water
3 eggs, lightly beaten
90 g/3¾ oz plain flour
FOR THE FILLING
450 ml/¾ pint double cream
25 g/1 oz preserved stem ginger, finely chopped
2 tablespoons syrup from the ginger jar
FOR THE TOPPNG
100 g/4 oz plain chocolate

Put the butter and water together in a large saucepan and bring slowly to the boil, making sure that the water does not boil before the fat is melted. But as soon as the fat *is* melted turn the heat up and bring the liquid to a rolling boil. Tip in all the flour at once and beat vigorously with a wooden spoon, drawing the pan off the heat as you do so. Keep beating until the mixture curls away from the sides of the pan and there are no more lumps. Allow the mixture to cool sufficiently to put your finger into it and then beat in the eggs one by one. The final mixture should be smooth and slightly shiny, and of a dropping consistency (that is, the mixture should fall reluctantly off the spoon, neither running off nor falling in a solid blob). Place the mixture in spoonfuls the size of ping-pong balls on a baking tray, leaving plenty of room between each spoonful to allow for expansion.

Bake the profiteroles in a moderately hot oven (200°C, 400°F, Gas Mark 6) until they are well risen and browned – about 20–30 minutes. Cut off the top third of each profiterole and scoop out any uncooked pastry from the inside.

Whip the double cream and add to it the chopped ginger and the ginger syrup. Use this to fill the bottom two-thirds of each profiterole. Replace the lids.

Put the chocolate in a small saucepan and stand it in another saucepan containing 5–7.5 cm/2–3 inches of hot water. Put over the heat and stir the chocolate gently until melted and smooth – don't let the chocolate boil. Spoon the melted chocolate carefully over the profiteroles and serve.

SERVES FOUR

MARMALADE APPLES

METRIC/IMPERIAL
100 g/4 oz butter
4 tablespoons golden syrup
2 tablespoons brown sugar
2 tablespoons marmalade (preferably dark and chunky)
1 heaped teaspoon mixed spice
8 eating apples, peeled, cored and quartered
juice and finely grated rind of 1 orange and 1 lemon
FOR THE CREAM
300 ml/½ pint double cream
2 egg whites
1 tablespoon castor sugar
300 ml/½ pint vanilla ice cream

In a heavy frying pan or shallow saucepan melt together the butter, syrup, brown sugar, marmalade and mixed spice. Add the quarters of apple and boil rapidly until the toffee is a good brown, and the apples are tender. Add the orange and lemon rind and juice and tip carefully into a shallow ovenproof dish. Keep hot.

Whip the cream until thick enough to hold its shape. Whisk the egg whites until stiff but not dry and beat the castor sugar into them. Fold the whipped cream and egg white mixture together. Serve the apples with the cream and ice cream handed separately.

SERVES FOUR TO FIVE

APRICOTS POACHED WITH KERNELS

METRIC/IMPERIAL
450 g/1 lb fresh firm apricots
300 ml/½ pint water
100 g/4 oz granulated sugar
TO SERVE
double cream *or* ice cream

Wash the apricots and cut them in half, removing the stones. Put the stones and apricot halves in a saucepan and add the water and the sugar. Bring up to the boil very slowly, allowing the sugar to melt before the water boils. Poach gently until the apricots are soft but not mushy. This may take as little as 10 minutes or as much as 30, depending on the ripeness of the fruit. Remove the stones and leave the apricots to cool in the sugar syrup.

When the apricots are cold, tip them with the syrup into a glass serving dish. Chill well. Crack the apricot stones with a hammer and take out the kernels. Chop them roughly and scatter them over the apricots before serving. Serve with cream or ice cream.

SERVES FOUR

FRIED MILK

A thin apricot sauce (see following recipe) is good with this, but it is very tasty on its own.

METRIC/IMPERIAL
300 ml/½ pint creamy milk
1 tablespoon granulated sugar
few drops vanilla essence
4 whole eggs
dried white breadcrumbs
butter for frying
cinnamon
castor sugar

Butter a square or oblong 1-litre/1½-pint ovenproof dish. Set the oven to moderate (160°C, 325°F, Gas Mark 3).

Heat the milk and sugar together, allow it to cool slightly and then add the vanilla essence. Lightly beat 3 of the eggs with a fork and pour on the hot milk. Mix well.

Strain this custard into the ovenproof dish or roasting tin and stand it in a larger roasting tin two thirds full of hot water. (This isn't strictly necessary but ensures a smooth custard.) Bake in the oven for 25–35 minutes or until the custard is set. Allow it to cool, then put in the refrigerator until really firmly set.

Beat the remaining egg in a small bowl and have ready the breadcrumbs in another one. Cut the custard into 5-cm/2-inch cubes and roll the cubes first in the egg mixture and then in the breadcrumbs.

Heat a good tablespoon of butter in the frying pan and when foaming add 2 or 3 custard cubes at a time. Fry gently, turning the blocks to brown all sides. Serve hot dusted with castor sugar and cinnamon.

SERVES FOUR

APRICOT SAUCE

This sauce is good with almost all custard or cake puddings, and with rice pudding, ice creams, profiteroles or meringues. An added splash of rum is a great idea for special occasions.

METRIC/IMPERIAL
100 g/4 oz sugar
300 ml/½ pint water
2 heaped tablespoons smooth apricot jam
juice of 1 lemon

Put everything together in a saucepan and simply heat slowly until smooth. For a thicker sauce boil rapidly for a few minutes.

Serve hot with cold puddings, and vice versa.

MAKES 300 ML/½ PINT

Not
So
Cheap...

Starters

EGG AND PEPPER SALAD

As a general rule I'm against 'arranged' salads. However, this one does look very pretty if the instructions are followed. But all the ingredients can simply be mixed in a bowl and will still look good and taste good.

METRIC/IMPERIAL
1 small green pepper, finely sliced
1 small red pepper, finely sliced
6 hard-boiled eggs
½ (56-g/2-oz) can anchovies
25 g/1 oz black olives
3 tomatoes, peeled and quartered
FOR THE DRESSING
4 tablespoons olive oil
1 tablespoon red wine vinegar
3 leaves basil, finely chopped
salt to taste
½ teaspoon freshly ground black pepper
good pinch of dry English mustard

To make the dressing combine the ingredients in a screw-top jar and shake well.

Put the slices of pepper, without any seeds, in a small saucepan and pour in enough boiling water to just cover them. Bring back to the boil and drain immediately. Dunk into cold water to set the colour, and then drain again.

On a flat dish with a good lip arrange the eggs: quarter them lengthways and lay them on their backs, yolk side up. Scatter the blanched green and red peppers all over the eggs. Use the anchovy fillets to lattice the top. Decorate with the olives, placed in the diagonal shapes formed by the lattice of anchovies. Surround with the tomatoes.

Just before serving give the dressing a good shake and spoon carefully all over the salad. SERVES FOUR TO FIVE

Not so cheap . . .

BASIC CHICKEN LIVER PÂTÉ

METRIC/IMPERIAL
175 g/6 oz butter
1 onion, sliced
225 g/8 oz chicken livers
½ clove garlic, crushed
salt and pepper
clarified butter (optional – see method)

In a frying pan melt 50 g/2 oz of the butter and add the sliced onion. Cook gently until the onion is transparent and soft. Turn up the heat and continue to cook the onion until it is just beginning to brown at the edges.

While the onion is cooking, trim any discoloured parts from the chicken livers as these are liable to taste bitter. Now add the chicken livers to the onion and butter in the pan and fry fairly briskly until the livers are brown on both sides, and cooked in the middle. Add the crushed garlic and plenty of salt and pepper. Now push this mixture, onions and all, through a sieve or blend it in an electric blender.

When the mixture is cold, or almost cold, beat in the rest of the butter. Turn the pâté into a small dish, or into individual ramekin dishes, and allow to set in the refrigerator. Serve with hot toast.

If the pâté is to be kept for any length of time it should be covered, once cold, with clarified butter. To clarify butter melt it without allowing it to burn and then strain it through a double thickness of muslin, or two J-cloths. When the clarified butter is cool, but still just runny, pour a thin layer all over the surface of the pâté. This will prevent the air getting at the pâté, and it should keep quite happily for a month or so in the refrigerator.

SERVES FOUR

TOMATO AND MOZZARELLA SALAD

METRIC/IMPERIAL
450 g/1 lb big ripe tomatoes (preferably the Mediterranean kind)
225 g/8 oz Mozzarella cheese
3 tablespoons olive oil
1 tablespoon white wine vinegar
salt and freshly ground black pepper
½ tablespoon chopped fresh basil
black olives

Peel the tomatoes (dunking them in boiling water for 5 seconds makes this easy) and slice them thickly across, discarding the stalk ends. Slice the Mozzarella cheese as thinly as you can. Arrange the tomatoes and cheese slices in alternate overlapping pieces on a flattish dish.

Make the dressing by putting the oil, vinegar, basil, and plenty of salt and pepper into a screwtop jar and shaking until you have a good emulsion. Spoon this carefully over the tomato and cheese and add a few black olives for decoration. SERVES FOUR

TARRAGON BAKED EGGS

METRIC/IMPERIAL
15 g/½ oz butter
4 eggs
4 tablespoons double cream
salt and freshly ground black pepper
8–10 tarragon leaves

Use the butter to grease 4 ramekin dishes very well. Break an egg into each dish, and spoon a tablespoon of cream over the top. Sprinkle with salt and pepper, and add a small pinch of chopped tarragon, or 2 whole tarragon leaves to each dish.

Stand the ramekin dishes in a roasting tin two thirds full of hot water and bake in a hot oven (220°C, 425°F, Gas Mark 7) for 12 minutes or until the whites are just set, and the yolks still runny. Alternatively, stand the ramekin dishes in a frying pan or shallow sauté pan half-filled with hot water and cover with a lid. Simmer gently on the top of the cooker until the whites are set – about 6 minutes. SERVES FOUR

Not so cheap . . .

AVOCADO PÂTÉ

METRIC/IMPERIAL
1 large ripe avocado
juice of ½ lemon
½ (142-ml/5-fl oz) carton soured cream (optional)
50 g/2 oz soft cream cheese
salt and pepper
1 clove garlic, crushed
2 rashers streaky bacon, with rind removed

Mash the avocado and mix in the lemon juice, soured cream, if used, and the cream cheese. Season well with salt and pepper, and crushed garlic.

Grill the bacon rashers until crisp and well browned. Allow them to cool and then crumble or chop them finely. Put the avocado mixture into a serving dish and sprinkle on the bacon bits.

If this pâté is to be made in advance the top layer is liable to discolour, despite the use of lemon juice. The answer to this is to spread a thin layer of soured cream, or cream cheese, or seasoned fresh cream all over the top of the dish to prevent the air getting to the avocado mixture

SERVES TWO OR FOUR

GLOOP SOUP

This rather unattractive name absolutely describes the texture of this soup, which is slippery, creamy and smooth. It is delicious, and must be the easiest soup in the world to make. It is important, however, to get proper jellied consommé. Recently some brands of consommé have been sold in cans with the legend 'Serve hot' on the label. This generally means that it will not set when cold. If the soup is liquid melt 7 g/¼ oz powdered gelatine in it and then allow to cool.

METRIC/IMPERIAL
1 (298-g/10½-oz) can jellied beef consommé
175 g/6 oz full-fat cream cheese

Keep back a quarter of the consommé for the top. Put the rest of the soup, and all the cream cheese, into an electric blender and whizz them together. Failing a blender, do it with a rotary beater or whisk.

Pour into small individual soup cups and allow to chill until set. Warm the remaining soup enough to be just runny, but by no means hot. Carefully pour a thin layer of clear consommé over the top of each soup cup. Chill again until set.

SERVES FOUR

FISH SOUP

This is an English version of the classic bouillabaisse, and none the worse for that. Surprisingly it contains chicken stock, which is not strictly necessary but is better than plain water. I have also made it very successfully with duck stock, but duck stock is not something one is likely to find in the fridge when it's needed!

METRIC/IMPERIAL
1.75 litres/3 pints chicken stock
1 kg/2 lb fish heads, skins and bones
handful of parsley
1 bay leaf
25 g/1 oz butter
1 large mild onion, finely chopped
1 large clove garlic, crushed
1 tablespoon tomato purée
1 kg/2 lb fresh white fish such as brill, haddock, hake, cod or whiting
4 fresh tomatoes, peeled and sliced
pinch of dried thyme
100 g/4 oz raw prawns, scampi or scallops
salt and freshly ground black pepper
FOR THE CROUTONS
2 slices white bread
oil for frying

Put the chicken stock, fish heads, skins and bones into a large saucepan and add half the parsley and the bay leaf. Bring to the boil and immediately turn the heat down. Simmer for 20 minutes exactly and then strain off the liquid into a jug and discard the fish heads, etc. Using the same saucepan, melt the butter and in it gently soften the chopped onion. When the onion is transparent, add the garlic and continue cooking for a further minute. Now add the tomato purée.

Cut the fish into small chunks and add them to the pan. Put on the lid and allow the fish to cook gently for 2–3 minutes. Add the strained stock, tomato slices and the pinch of thyme. Bring to simmering point and add the raw shellfish. Simmer for 3–5 minutes more or until the fish and shellfish are just tender.

Remove the crusts and cut the bread into triangular quarters. Fry in hot oil until crisp and brown. Chop the rest of the parsley and dip each triangular croûton into it. Hand round with the soup.

SERVES SIX

BAKED MUSSELS PROVENÇALE

METRIC/IMPERIAL
1.75 kg/4 lb or 2 litres/4 pints fresh live mussels
1 onion, roughly chopped
1 bay leaf
150 ml/¼ pint water
3 tablespoons finely chopped parsley
150 g/5 oz butter, softened
1 clove garlic, crushed
1 tablespoon finely chopped shallot *or* onion
FOR THE TOPPING
25 g/1 oz Gruyère cheese, finely grated
25 g/1 oz dried breadcrumbs (preferably baked brown)

Soak the mussels in fresh water to remove any sand, then scrub them well, throwing away cracked ones or ones which will not shut when tapped on the sink. Remove their 'beards' and put the mussels into a large saucepan with the chopped onion, bay leaf and water. Cover with the lid and cook over a moderate heat, shaking the pan occasionally, until all the mussels have opened – 3 minutes is usually enough. Open the shells completely, throwing away the top shell of each mussel. Remove the rubbery band from the mussels, but leave them in the bottom shell.

Preheat the oven to moderately hot (190°C, 375°F, Gas Mark 5) while you make the garlic butter: mix together the parsley, butter, crushed garlic and the finely chopped shallot and beat to a paste. Spread each mussel with this and place the shells, containing the buttered mussels, on a large ovenproof dish or on four smaller ones. Mix the cheese and breadcrumbs together and sprinkle carefully over the top. Bake the mussels in the oven until bubbly and just beginning to brown – about 10 minutes.

SERVES SIX

MARINATED KIPPER FILLETS

METRIC/IMPERIAL
225 g/8 oz boned kipper fillets (frozen is fine)
4 tablespoons salad oil
juice of 1 small lemon
1 medium mild onion, finely sliced
1 bay leaf
freshly ground black pepper

If the kipper fillets are frozen allow them to thaw before you begin, then skin the fillets and put them in a deepish dish. Add everything else, turning the fillets so that they are well coated in oil and lemon juice.

Leave them in the fridge (covered with polythene wrap or some such to prevent everything else in the fridge tasting of kippers) for as long as you can – 3 days is not too long, and 12 hours is not really enough. Serve the kipper fillets with hot toast fingers.

SERVES FOUR

TARAMASALATA

METRIC/IMPERIAL
1 slice white bread
1 large clove garlic, crushed
225 g/8 oz smoked soft cod's roe, skinned
about 300 ml/½ pint salad oil
freshly ground white pepper
about 3 tablespoons lemon juice

Wet the bread and squeeze it out so that it is moist but not sopping. Put it in a bowl with the crushed garlic and the cod's roe. Preferably with an electric mixer, but failing that with a wooden spoon, beat the roes until smooth. Gradually add the oil, as though you were making mayonnaise (that is, drip by drip at first, beating each dribble of oil in before you add the next). Gradually the cod's roe mixture will become creamier and thicker, and now you can add the oil more boldly.

Add as much oil as you like – the more oil you add the creamier and blander will be the taste. Very salty roe needs more oil than very mild roe. Season with the pepper and plenty of lemon juice. Serve with hot toast.

SERVES FOUR

AUBERGINE CAVIAR

This recipe has a misleading name, as many people think it must be something to do with caviar. But it isn't.

METRIC/IMPERIAL
1 large aubergine
salt and freshly ground black pepper
1 clove garlic, crushed
juice of 1 small lemon
about 175 ml/6 fl oz olive oil
chopped parsley (optional)

Heat the grill until blazing hot and grill the aubergine, unskinned, all over until the skin is completely black and the flesh of the aubergine feels soft when pierced with a skewer. Alternatively, cook the aubergine whole in a hot oven.

Allow the aubergine to cool enough to handle and then skin it, putting the pulpy flesh into a bowl. Season the flesh with salt, pepper, crushed garlic and lemon juice. Beat the mixture well with a wooden spoon, or put it into an electric blender.

When you have an absolutely smooth paste gradually beat in the oil. It is important that the oil is added slowly at first, because you are aiming for a mayonnaise-like emulsion. If you add the oil too fast it may curdle and separate. Add as much oil as you like, beating continuously. The more oil you add the milder and thicker the mixture will be.

It must be confessed that the look of this dip or paste is not very attractive. So serve it in a pretty dish, perhaps scattered with chopped parsley. It is delicious with toast.

SERVES FOUR

Main Courses

HADDOCK DUGLÉRÉ

METRIC/IMPERIAL

4 fresh skinned haddock fillets, weighing about 175 g/6 oz each, and
the skin, head and bones of the fish (or any other bones, etc.)

450 ml/¾ pint water

150 ml/¼ pint white wine

3 slices onion

3 slices carrot

3 chunks celery

1 bay leaf

handful of parsley

salt and pepper

FOR THE SAUCE

25 g/1 oz butter

25 g/1 oz flour

3 large tomatoes, peeled

1 tablespoon chopped chives

150 ml/¼ pint single cream

Put the fish fillets into a roasting tin and cover them with the fish
skins, bones, etc. Add the water and wine and sink the onion, carrot,
celery, bay leaf and the parsley stalks (but not all the leaves) in it.
Add salt and pepper. Cover the roasting tin with foil or greaseproof
paper and bake in a moderate oven (180°C, 350°F, Gas Mark 4) for
15–20 minutes or until the fish is cooked. Lift out the fillets, drain
well and lay them in a serving dish. Cover with the foil to stop them
drying out and set aside. Reserve the cooking liquid.

To make the sauce: melt the butter in a saucepan and when
foaming stir in the flour. Stir for a further minute and then strain on
450 ml/¾ pint of the cooking liquid saved from the roasting tin. Stir
the sauce until well blended and smooth, and boiling. Allow to
simmer for 3 or 4 minutes.

Cut the tomatoes into quarters, remove the seeds and cut each quarter into thin slivers. Chop the parsley leaves. Put the tomato, parsley, chives and cream into the sauce and stir, without boiling, to reheat. Once hot, pour immediately over the fish and serve at once.

SERVES FOUR

STUFFED FILLETS OF PLAICE WITH COURGETTES

METRIC/IMPERIAL
1 onion, finely chopped
butter for frying
175 g/6 oz mushrooms, finely chopped
450 g/1 lb courgettes
salt and freshly ground black pepper
8 fillets of plaice, skinned
lemon juice
1 tablespoon split almonds

Start with the mushroom *farce:* soften the onion over moderate heat in about 1 tablespoon of butter. When the onion is transparent-looking add the chopped mushrooms and fry until you have a soft, reduced mixture. Tip this into a bowl and allow to cool.

Set the oven to moderately hot (200°C, 400°F, Gas Mark 6). Season the mushroom mixture well with salt and pepper and divide it between the eight plaice fillets. Fold these in half lengthways over the mushroom mixture with the skinned side of the fish inside. Put the plaice rolls side by side in a buttered flameproof dish and cover with foil. Bake in the oven for 20 minutes or until the fish feels firm to the touch and a thin skewer will glide easly through the thickest part of them.

Meanwhile prepare the courgettes. Do not peel them but using a large-gauge cheese grater or vegetable shredder grate them coarsely and then in a large frying pan melt 2 tablespoons of butter and tip in the courgettes. Shake the pan and stir and turn the contents frequently, frying over a moderate heat so that the courgettes soften without browning. When buttery and soft, season with salt and pepper and sprinkle with lemon juice, then spread them on a heated serving dish. Melt a little more butter in the frying pan and add the almonds. Fry them fast until brown.

Once the fish is cooked put the stuffed fish rolls on the top of the courgettes and scatter the fried almonds over them. Serve at once.

SERVES FOUR

COULIBIAC

This is a sort of Russian fish pie, normally made with puff pastry (frozen is fine) and containing fish. Cooked fresh salmon is undoubtedly the best, but very expensive, and can be replaced with canned salmon or other cooked fish, or poached chicken.

METRIC/IMPERIAL
225 g/8 oz puff pastry
(see page 169 *or* use frozen)
350 g/12 oz cooked fresh salmon
50 g/2 oz butter
1 onion, finely chopped
50 g/2 oz mushrooms, sliced
100 g/4 oz long-grain rice, boiled (weighed before cooking)
2 hard-boiled eggs, sliced
1 tablespoon chopped parsley
juice of ½ lemon
salt and freshly ground black pepper
little beaten egg

Roll a third of the pastry out into a large rectangle about 20 cm/ 8 inches long and 7.5 cm/3 inches wide. Put it on a wet baking tray and leave for 10 minutes to relax. Then prick it all over with a fork and bake in a moderately hot oven (200°C, 400°F, Gas Mark 6) until very crisp and brown. Turn it over and put it back in the oven for a further 2 minutes to ensure there is no soggy patch underneath. Baking will take 15–20 minutes. Cool this pastry base on a wire rack, and swish the baking tray under cold water to get it cold too.

Bone the salmon and flake it into a large bowl. Melt the butter in a frying pan and fry the finely chopped onion until soft, then add the mushrooms and fry for a further minute or so. Tip this mixture on top of the salmon. Add the boiled rice, the eggs, parsley and lemon juice, and season well with salt and pepper.

Return the crisp pastry base to the now cold (and dried) baking tray and pile the salmon mixture on to it, shaping into a smooth mound with your hands. Roll the remaining pastry out into a very thin 'blanket' large enough to cover the salmon mixture and its base, leaving a 1-cm/½-inch border to tuck under. (It is better to make too big a blanket than to try to stretch the pastry to fit.) Cut off any excess pastry and use the trimming to make leaves or shapes to decorate the top of the pie.

Brush all over with beaten egg, fixing the decoration on as you go, and brushing again with beaten egg when it is in place. Return to the oven and cook until the pastry is brown and the filling reheated – about 20 minutes. Serve hot or cold with a green salad.

SERVES FOUR TO FIVE

FISH KEBABS

METRIC/IMPERIAL
450 g/1 lb firm white fish, preferably turbot, hake, or haddock
225 g/8 oz streaky bacon, with rind removed
225 g/8 oz button mushrooms
50 g/2 oz butter, melted
freshly ground black pepper
½ tablespoon chopped fennel (the herb, not the vegetable)
juice of 1 lemon

Cut the fish into 2.5-cm/1-inch cubes and wrap each piece in streaky bacon. Skewer the bacon and fish alternately with the button mushrooms on 4 short metal or wooden skewers.

Heat the grill. Brush the kebabs all over with melted butter and season well with pepper. Do not add salt as the bacon will provide plenty. Sprinkle over half the chopped fennel and grill under high heat. Turn the kebabs as they grill so that they are evenly browned on all sides. Just before serving sprinkle with the lemon juice and the rest of the chopped fennel.

SERVES TWO OR FOUR

SPAGHETTI BOLOGNESE

METRIC/IMPERIAL
225 g/8 oz spaghetti
FOR THE SAUCE
50 g/2 oz chicken livers (optional, but good)
6 rashers streaky bacon, with rind removed
beef dripping for frying
225 g/8 oz minced beef
15 g/½ oz butter
1 stick celery, very finely chopped
1 onion, finely chopped
100 g/4 oz diced mushrooms *or* chopped mushrooms peelings *or*
stalks
1 clove garlic, crushed
3 tablespoons Madeira
300 ml/½ pint beef stock
2 tablespoons tomato purée
1 (227-g/8-oz) can peeled Italian tomatoes
salt and freshly ground black pepper
good pinch of dried oregano
TO SERVE
freshly grated Parmesan cheese

If you are using the chicken livers (they add richness to the sauce, but many people don't bother with them) trim off any discoloured parts which might make the sauce bitter. In a heavy-bottomed saucepan fry the bacon in its own fat until it is lightly brown all over. Add the dripping, reheat, and briskly fry the chicken livers in it until they are brown on both sides, but not necessarily cooked inside. Lift out the livers and the bacon with a perforated spoon.

Add a little more dripping to the saucepan if necessary and fry the minced beef, half at a time (putting the whole lot in at once lowers the temperature too much, with the result that the meat stews rather than fries). Lift out the meat, add the butter to the pan and put into it the chopped celery and onion. Stir well, scratching up any bits from the bottom. Cook slowly until the vegetables are soft and just beginning to colour. Add the chopped mushroom and the garlic and cook for a further minute or so. Then put back the meat. Add the wine, stock, tomato purée and the tomatoes with their juices. Season with salt, pepper and oregano and bring up to the boil.

Turn the heat down and simmer very gently for 45 minutes or so until the meat is absolutely tender (stewing beef obviously takes

107

longer than expensive steak). When the meat is tender the sauce should have a syrupy consistency, being thick but runny. If too thin, boil it rapidly until the right consistency is reached; if too thick, and sticking to the bottom of the pan, add water.

To cook the spaghetti: bring a large pan of salted water to the boil and plunge the spaghetti into it, pushing the pasta under the water as it softens. Cook for 10–12 minutes (testing after 10 minutes), or until the spaghetti is tender but not mushy. Tip into a colander and run plenty of hot water through to wash off any excess starch. Leave to drain for a minute or two and then return it to the rinsed-out saucepan with 2 teaspoons or so of oil – enough to thoroughly grease the spaghetti. Tip into a hot bowl or serving dish and hand the sauce separately.

Occasionally spaghetti bolognese is served with the sauce poured over the spaghetti. But in either event, hand the grated cheese separately, as not everyone likes it.

SERVES FOUR

BRISKET OF BEEF WITH OYSTER STUFFING

Brisket of beef is a little fatty even when cooked very slowly. To counteract this serve with plenty of mashed potatoes. This is a traditional English recipe hardly ever seen today. It well repays the effort involved and is fairly economical.

METRIC/IMPERIAL
1.75 kg/4 lb boned brisket of beef
3 rashers streaky bacon, finely chopped
2 tablespoons chopped parsley
6 oysters, finely chopped (frozen oysters are fine)
¼ teaspoon nutmeg
salt and freshly ground black pepper
about 15 g/½ oz flour
300 ml/½ pint red wine
300 ml/½ pint beef stock

Lay the beef flat on the board, skin side down. Mix together the bacon, parsley, oysters, half the nutmeg, a good pinch of salt and plenty of freshly ground black pepper. Spread this mixture over the brisket, then roll it up from the thin end and tie securely with pieces of string at 3.5-cm/1½-inch intervals. Put the brisket into a roasting

tin and dredge it well with the flour. Pour in the wine and the stock
and put the roasting tin over direct heat until the liquid is boiling.
Transfer to a cool oven (150°C, 300°F, Gas Mark 2) and bake for 4
hours or until the beef is really tender. Put the beef on a warmed
serving dish and remove the pieces of string. Keep warm.

Skim the fat off the juices in the roasting tin and spoon the juices
over the meat.

SERVES EIGHT TO TEN

BEEF GOULASH

METRIC/IMPERIAL
450 g/1 lb good chuck steak, cut into largish cubes
2 tablespoons beef dripping
3 medium onions, sliced
1 large clove garlic, crushed
1–2 tablespoons paprika
2 teaspoons flour
1 (425-g/15-oz) can peeled tomatoes
450 ml/¾ pint stock
1 teaspoon caraway seeds
salt and pepper
bunch of herbs (sprig of parsley, 1 bay leaf, sprig of thyme) tied
together with string
450 g/1 lb small waxy potatoes, peeled
1 tablespoon tomato purée
1 (142-ml/5-fl oz) carton soured cream
TO SERVE
chopped parsley *or* shreds cooked red pepper

In a heavy saucepan fry the cubes of beef in the dripping until well
browned all over. When they are done remove them with a
perforated spoon to a plate. Now put the onions and the garlic into
the pan, turn down the heat and cook slowly until soft and evenly
coloured. Return the meat to the pan and add the paprika (1–2
tablespoons according to taste). Stir over the heat for a few seconds,
then add the flour and stir well. Now add the canned tomatoes, the
stock, caraway seeds and plenty of salt and pepper and put in the
bunch of herbs. Stir very well, making sure that the tomatoes are
distributed throughout the stew while bringing the stew to the boil.
Cover the pan and simmer gently until the meat is tender – about 2
hours. Alternatively, cook for 2½ hours in a cool oven (150°C,

300°F, Gas Mark 2).

When you feel the meat is nearly cooked (perhaps after 1½ hours) add the peeled potatoes, the tomato purée and more salt and pepper if necessary. Continue cooking until the potatoes are soft and the meat is tender. With a perforated spoon lift all the solid ingredients out of the stew and put into a serving dish. Discard the herbs. Boil the remaining liquid in the pan until reduced to a thick rich sauce, stirring occasionally to prevent burning on the bottom of the pan. Pour over the meat and spoon blobs of soured cream on top. Scatter the chopped parsley or finely shredded cooked red pepper on top and serve at once.

SERVES FOUR TO FIVE

BOLLITO

This is simply an Italian version of boiled beef, or very often boiled mixed meats. A bollito can include almost anything, and the beef can be salted or not as preferred. A bollito is not much good as a dish for 4 people – there will be far too much. But it is a marvellous party dish for 10 people or more.

METRIC/IMPERIAL
1.25–1.5 kg/2½–3 lb brisket or other boiling joint of
fresh, unsalted beef
1 bay leaf
handful of parsley stalks
sprig of fresh thyme
1 beef stock cube
1 small bacon joint (about 675–900 g/1½–2 lb)
1 (1.75-kg/4-lb) chicken *or* a small boiling fowl
450 g/1 lb carrots, peeled
12 button onions, peeled
3 or 4 sticks celery, cut into chunks
1 pork boiling sausage (or Polish boiling ring)
salt and freshly ground black pepper

Start with whatever is likely to take longest to boil – in this case the boiling beef or brisket. Put it in a saucepan large enough to hold finally all the ingredients, and cover with water. Add the bay leaf, parsley stalks and thyme, tied together with string, and the beef stock cube. Bring up to the boil, turn down the heat, put on the lid and simmer very gently for 30 minutes. Now add the bacon joint, topping up with more water if necessary.

Thirty minutes later add the chicken and the vegetables, again adding sufficient water to almost cover the meats. Continue simmering very gently for 80 minutes. Then add the boiling sausage and continue cooking until everything is tender – another 20 minutes or so. If you find that the beef, for example, is tender before the bacon is, or the chicken cooks more quickly than you had expected, simply lift out the cooked meats, put them on a plate and cover them with foil or plastic wrap to stop them steaming dry. They can be added to the pan when everything else is cooked.

When everything is tender skim off any fat and remove the herbs. Add salt and pepper if necessary.

To serve the bollito, provide everybody with large old-fashioned soup plates rather than dinner plates, or with soup bowls *and* dinner plates. The soup is eaten at the same time as the meat in some parts of Italy. Do as you prefer.

SERVES TEN

BEEF CARBONNADE

METRIC/IMPERIAL
1 tablespoon beef dripping
1 kg/2 lb chuck steak, cut into large chunks
300 ml/½ pint Guinness or other brown stout
3 onions, roughly sliced
½ tablespoon brown sugar
1 tablespoon flour
1 clove garlic, crushed
1 teaspoon wine vinegar *or* lemon juice
sprig of thyme
1 bay leaf
bunch of parsley
pinch of nutmeg
salt and freshly ground black pepper
FOR THE TOPPING
2 slices bread spread with mustard

Melt the dripping in a heavy frying pan and fry the meat, 2 or 3 pieces at a time, until well browned all over. Put them into a flameproof casserole as they are done. If the pan becomes very dry and is in danger of burning add a little Guinness to it, swish the juices around, and tip them into the casserole with the meat.

When the meat is all done fry the onions in the same pan, adding the sugar when they are half cooked. As the sugar melts it will form a pale toffee. When this happens tip the onions and toffee juices into the casserole. Sprinkle the flour on top of the onions and meat and mix well. Pour in the Guinness, add the garlic and enough water, if necessary, to come about half way up the meat. Add the wine vinegar, the herbs, tied together with string, the nutmeg and plenty of salt and pepper. Bring to the boil.

Cover the casserole with a well-fitting lid and cook in a cool oven (150°C, 300°F, Gas Mark 2) for 2½–2¾ hours or until the meat is really tender. Take off the lid, remove the herbs and put the slices of mustard-covered bread on top of the stew, mustard side up. The bread will absorb the beef fat which will have come out of the meat during cooking. Return the dish to the oven for 15 minutes or so until the bread is brown and crisp.

SERVES FOUR

CHOUCROUTE GARNI

This is a dish found all over France, particularly in the Alsace region, where the German influence is very strong. Almost any smoked sausage can go into it but this is a fairly typical example.

METRIC/IMPERIAL
450 g/1 lb sauerkraut
1 glass white wine
freshly ground black pepper
5–7.5-cm/2–3-inch garlic sausage, peeled and coarsely sliced
2 pork frankfurters, cut in half
2 gammon steaks, cut in half
2–3 juniper berries, crushed (optional)
350 g/12 oz small boiled potatoes
2 hard-boiled eggs
1 teaspoon chopped parsley

Drain the sauerkraut and put it into a large heavy saucepan. Add the wine, and grind in plenty of black pepper. On top of the sauerkraut lay the slices of garlic sausage, the frankfurters and gammon steaks. Add the crushed juniper berries if you are using them. Cover the pan very tightly and set over a gentle heat to barely simmer for 25 minutes or until the gammon is tender.

Add the boiled potatoes and continue simmering until they are hot. Quarter the hard-boiled eggs and heat them by adding to the pan for a further 3–4 minutes.

To dish the choucroute: arrange the sauerkraut on the bottom of a large, shallow heated platter with everything else on top, except the potatoes which should surround the dish, or be piled to one side of the sauerkraut. Just before serving, scatter the chopped parsley all over.

SERVES SIX

STUFFED ROAST PORK WITH APRICOT AND DATE STUFFING

METRIC/IMPERIAL
2-kg/4½-lb piece of boned loin of pork with both crackling and belly flap still attached
salt
about 1 tablespoon flour
300 ml/½ pint stock or water
FOR THE STUFFING
1 small onion, chopped
1 tablespoon butter
65 g/2½ oz fresh white breadcrumbs
25 g/1 oz chopped dried apricots (not soaked)
1 tablespoon hazelnuts, chopped
12 dates, chopped
juice of ½ lemon
salt and pepper
beaten egg

First make the stuffing: fry the onion slowly in the butter until just turning colour. Add all the other ingredients, using just enough egg to bind the mixture together.

Make sure the crackling is evenly and well scored by the butcher. If it is not, cut parallel lines through the outer skin all over it with a sharp kitchen knife, Stanley knife or razor blade.

Lay the loin of pork, crackling side down, on a board. Spread the stuffing on the meat and roll up, tying pieces of string at 2.5-cm/ 1-inch intervals round the joint to hold it together. Put the pork, crackling side up, in a roasting tin and sprinkle salt lightly but evenly all over it to make the crackling bubbly and crisp. Heat the oven to hot (220°C, 425°F, Gas Mark 7), and when hot put in the pork. After 45 minutes reduce the heat to moderately hot (200°C, 400°F, Gas

Mark 6), and continue to roast, basting once or twice, until the meat is tender and the crackling crisp and brown, about 1¾–2 hours.

Lift the meat out on to a serving dish and keep warm.

Skim the fat from the roasting tin. Sprinkle enough flour into the juices in the pan to absorb what remains of the fat, stir in the stock or water and stir or whisk steadily while bringing to the boil. Taste and add salt and pepper if necessary. Strain into a gravy boat and serve with the roast pork.

SERVES SIX TO EIGHT

STUFFED PORK FILLETS IN CIDER

METRIC/IMPERIAL
2 small pork fillets
8 prunes, soaked overnight
about 1 tablespoon butter
1 medium onion, finely chopped
1 small cooking apple, peeled, cored and chopped
1 dessert apple, peeled, cored and chopped
300 ml/½ pint cider
salt and freshly ground black pepper
15 g/½ oz butter and 15 g/½ oz flour mixed together to a paste

Cut each pork fillet into four pieces. Stone the prunes. Make a small cut in each chunk of pork and push a prune into it, burying the prune as far as possible in the pork flesh. Melt the butter in a frying pan and in it brown the pork pieces fairly fast until well covered on all sides. Lift the pieces into a casserole as they are browned. Then soften the chopped onion in the butter in the frying pan, adding more if necessary. Add the chopped apple, both dessert and cooking, to the onion in the pan and pour in the cider. Boil up and tip over the pork fillets in the casserole. Grind some black pepper over the top, and add a sprinkling of salt. Cover the casserole and bake in a moderate oven (180°C, 350°F, Gas Mark 4) until the pork is very tender, about 40 minutes.

Lift the chunks of pork and the apple on to a serving dish and put the juices from the casserole back into the frying pan. Alternatively, if the casserole can go on direct heat simply transfer it to the top of the stove. Boil the juices in the frying pan or casserole and slowly whisk small pieces of the butter and flour mixture into it. When it is the consistency of thin cream, allow it to simmer for 1 minute, then taste for seasoning and add more salt and pepper if necessary. Pour over the pork and serve.

SERVES FOUR

MUSTARD PORK CHOPS

METRIC/IMPERIAL
4 pork chops
1 teaspoon butter
2 teaspoons celery seed
1 tablespoon light French mustard (Dijon)
1 (142-ml/5-fl oz) carton yogurt
salt and freshly ground black pepper
squeeze of lemon
TO SERVE
watercress

Cut the outer skin from the chops and then using a sharp knife or scissors, snip through the fat towards the meat at 1-cm/½-inch intervals. Melt the butter in a frying pan and brown the chops quickly on both sides, then lower the heat and fry gently until cooked through. Lift the chops on to a serving dish and arrange them attractively.

Tip off any fat from the frying pan and put the pan back, unwashed, on to the heat. In it fry the celery seed for half a minute, then stir in the French mustard and yogurt. Add salt and pepper to taste and a squeeze of lemon juice. Pour over the pork chops, garnish them with the sprigs of watercress and serve at once.

SERVES FOUR

STUFFED VEAL PARCELS

METRIC/IMPERIAL
4 (100-g/4-oz) veal escalopes
butter
lemon juice
FOR THE FILLING
450 g/1 lb fresh spinach or young kale leaves
75 g/3 oz button mushrooms, finely sliced
15 g/½ oz butter
50 g/2 oz Gruyère cheese, cut in small cubes
2 tablespoons cream
salt and pepper

Wash the spinach or kale and put it, still wet, into a saucepan over gentle heat and cook, covered, very briefly until soft but still bright green. Squeeze dry, and chop roughly. Fry the mushrooms in the butter, then mix with the spinach, cheese, and cream, and season well with salt and pepper. Allow to cool.

Put the veal escalopes between two sheets of plastic wrap and, with a rolling pin, beat out until thin and flat. Put a spoonful of the cold spinach mixture on to each escalope and wrap them up like a parcel, tying them with cotton to stop them unravelling. Fry the parcels slowly in butter until pale brown on both sides. Cover the pan and cook for a further five minutes a side or until tender. Put them on a warm serving dish, squeeze a little lemon juice into the frying pan, and boil up. Pour, sizzling, over the veal parcels and serve at once.

SERVES FOUR

VEAL FLORENTINE

METRIC/IMPERIAL
65 g/2½ oz butter
4 small veal escalopes, beaten thin
1 clove garlic, crushed
225 g/8 oz tomatoes, peeled and sliced
450 g/1 lb fresh or 1 (142-g/5-oz) packet frozen leaf spinach
salt and freshly ground black pepper
25 g/1 oz plain flour
450 ml/¾ pint creamy milk
65 g/2½ oz Gruyère cheese, grated
1 tablespoon fresh breadcrumbs

Melt 25 g/1 oz of the butter in a frying pan and in it quickly brown the veal on both sides. Lift out the slices and put them on a plate. Fry the crushed garlic in the pan for half a minute or so and then add the tomatoes. Fry the tomatoes rather fast until they are just beginning to brown, but still firm rather than mushy. Lay the tomatoes in the bottom of a pie dish. Cut the veal into thin strips and put it on top of the tomatoes.

Cook the spinach until reduced in bulk but still bright green; follow the manufacturer's instructions for frozen spinach. If fresh, wash the leaves well, pull out any really tough stalks and cook the leaves in a coverd saucepan with not more than 3 tablespoons of water and a pinch of salt for 3–4 minutes. Squeeze all the moisture out of the spinach leaves and chop them roughly on a board. Return them to the dry saucepan and add 15 g/½ oz of the butter. Toss well, adding freshly ground black pepper, and salt if necessary. When the spinach is well coated, spread it on top of the veal slices in the dish.

To make the cheese sauce: melt the remaining butter (25 g/1 oz) and stir in the flour. Cook over a gentle heat until the butter foams, then draw off the heat. Stir in the milk, return to the heat and stir until boiling. Season with salt and pepper and add 50 g/2 oz of the grated Gruyère cheese, taking care that the sauce does not boil again. Once the cheese has melted pour the sauce over the spinach.

Mix the breadcrumbs with the remaining 15 g/½ oz of Gruyère cheese and sprinkle evenly over the top of the dish. Reheat in a hot oven (220°C, 425°F, Gas Mark 7) until the sauce is bubbly, and the top just beginning to brown.

SERVES FOUR

SPICY STUFFED LAMB

METRIC/IMPERIAL
1.5 kg/3½ lb shoulder of lamb, boned
FOR THE STUFFING
2 rashers streaky bacon, with rind removed
25 g/1 oz butter
100 g/4 oz chicken livers, with discoloured parts removed, sliced
1 large onion, finely chopped
100 g/4 oz mushrooms, sliced
1 large clove garlic, crushed
1 tablespoon mixed chopped fresh herbs
(such as thyme, parsley and marjoram)
grated rind of ½ lemon
25 g/1 oz sultanas
salt and freshly ground black pepper
pinch each of nutmeg and turmeric
175 g/6 oz cooked long-grain rice
FOR THE GRAVY
2 teaspoons flour
1 tablespoon tomato purée
300 ml/½ pint stock or water

To make the stuffing: dice the bacon, melt a little of the butter in a frying pan and add the bacon to it. Fry fairly fast until the bacon bits are turning brown, then add the chicken liver.

Fry fast until brown then, using a perforated spoon, lift the bacon and liver from the pan. Now add the rest of the butter to the pan and fry the chopped onion in it. When the onion is soft and beginning to colour, add the mushrooms and the garlic. Stir well and cook for 1 minute, then add the tablespoon of herbs, the grated lemon rind and the sultanas. Season with salt, pepper and a pinch each of nutmeg and turmeric.

Fork the onion and mushroom mixture into the rice and add the bacon and liver. Put the stuffing into the shoulder of lamb, sewing up the edges with string. Put the lamb into a roasting tin, brush it with a little melted butter and roast in a moderately hot oven (200°C, 400°F, Gas Mark 6) for about 1¼ hours, basting occasionally.

To make the gravy: lift the meat from the tin and pour off most of the fat. Keep all the juices and about a tablespoon of fat. Mix the flour into this, scraping the bottom of the roasting tin well to loosen any stuck sediment. Stir in the tomato purée and the stock. Bring to the boil, stirring. Add salt and pepper if necessary.

SERVES FOUR TO SIX

LAMB CURRY

This dish is a true Indian curry, rather dry, and served with fresh yogurt. It bears no resemblance to the English type of curry where there is more sauce than meat and the sauce is thickened with flour – something seldom done in India.

METRIC/IMPERIAL
50 g/2 oz ghee or clarified butter
2 onions, sliced
1 large clove garlic, crushed
pinch of cinnamon
1 teaspoon nutmeg
1 teaspoon ground cardamom
1 teaspoon ground turmeric
1 teaspoon ground coriander
pinch of cumin seeds
1 kg/2 lb lean lamb, cut into cubes
1 tablespoon tomato purée
2 teaspoons mango chutney
1 (142-ml/5-fl oz) carton plain yogurt

Heat the clarified butter or ghee in a heavy-bottomed saucepan and in it fry the onion slices until barely brown. Add the garlic and all the spices. Stir over gentle heat for 4 minutes. Add the meat, tomato purée and chutney, and mix well. Pour in a teacup of water and the yogurt and stir until simmering. Cover and cook very gently until the meat is tender – about 1¾ hours.

By now the sauce should be much reduced, just enough to coat the meat nicely. If it is too liquid lift out the meat and boil the sauce rapidly until the desired consistency is reached. Serve with plain boiled rice.

SERVES FOUR

LAMB CHOPS WITH HARICOT BEANS

METRIC/IMPERIAL
350 g/12 oz dried haricot beans
50 g/2 oz butter
1 large onion, sliced
1 clove garlic, crushed
2 teaspoons tomato purée
salt and pepper
4 butterfly chops *or* 8 loin of lamb chops,
cut into 4 double-thick chops (each containing 2 bones)
sprig of rosemary
3 tomatoes, peeled and quartered
1 tablespoon chopped parsley
squeeze of lemon juice

Start with the beans. If you have time soak them in cold water overnight. If not, pour hot water over them and leave for 3–4 hours or until they feel softened when tested between the fingers.

In a heavy frying pan melt half the butter and fry the onion slices until soft and just beginning to colour. Add the garlic and fry for a further minute. Tip the garlic and onion, and any butter, into a casserole and add the drained haricot beans. Add the tomato purée, salt and pepper, and enough water to come three-quarters of the way up the beans. Stir the beans briskly with a fork and cover well with a lid, or with greaseproof paper and foil tied down well. Bake in a moderate oven (180°C, 350°F, Gas Mark 4) until the beans have absorbed most of the water and are tender. During the cooking process it helps a lot if you gently stir the beans so that the bottom ones get to the top and vice versa. They will take about 2½ hours.

Meanwhile, prepare the chops if not already prepared by your butcher. With a short sharp knife carefully remove both bones from each double chop. You should now have a thick steaklike piece of meat, oval-shaped. Carefully slice through this meat horizontally as if to make 2 thin steaks, but do not slice right to the edge – cut from the rounded side of the chop towards the flatter side and stop about 1 cm/½ inch before the end. Now open the meat out like a book and flatten it with your hands, so that you will have a butterfly-shaped piece of meat. Sprinkle on both sides with a few rosemary leaves, roughly chopped, and plenty of freshly ground black pepper. Press the seasonings well into the meat. Leave chops in the opened-up position until ready to fry them.

When the beans are cooked and tender, heat the rest of the butter in the frying pan until foaming. Lay in the butterfly chops. Brown them fairly fast at first, on both sides, and then turn the heat down and cook until the chops are well browned all over, but still pink and moist in the middle.

To serve, pile the cooked beans in the middle of a warmed platter and surround with the butterfly chops. Keep warm. Put the quartered tomatoes into the frying pan with the chopped parsley and the squeeze of lemon juice (and a little more butter if necessary – you want about a tablespoon of lamb juices and fat in the pan). Heat rapidly until foaming and pour over the chops just before taking them to the table.

SERVES FOUR

MOUSSAKA

*There is great debate among aficionados of moussaka about
whether it should have a custard-like top or not. Classic
recipes omit this egg and cream mixture but I have eaten
moussaka all over Greece with the frowned-upon topping, and I
must say I think it the better for it.*

METRIC/IMPERIAL
1 large aubergine, thickly sliced
salt and pepper
olive oil
1 large onion, chopped
675 g/1½ lb lean raw lamb or mutton, minced
1 clove garlic, crushed
225 g/8 oz tomatoes, peeled
150 ml/¼ pint white wine
150 ml/¼ pint water
handful of parsley, chopped
pinch of ground nutmeg
1 large boiled potato, finely sliced
FOR THE TOPPING
15 g/½ oz butter
15 g/½ oz flour
1 bay leaf
300 ml/½ pint milk
1 egg yolk
2 tablespoons cream
50 g/2 oz cheese such as Cheddar, grated
1 tablespoon dried white breadcrumbs

Lightly sprinkle the aubergine slices on both sides with salt. Leave
for 30 minutes then rinse well and pat dry.

In a large heavy-bottomed saucepan heat the oil and add to it the
chopped onion. Cook slowly until the onion goes first soft and then
very slightly brown. Add the meat and the garlic and stir over a
moderate heat for a further 5 minutes or so until all the lamb is well
browned. Chop the tomatoes and put them into the meat, seeds and
all. Add the white wine, water, chopped parsley, salt and pepper
and the nutmeg and stir well. Set over a gentle heat and cook until
most of the liquid has evaporated, and the meat is tender – about 1
hour.

Heat a little more oil (about 2 tablespoons) in a large heavy frying pan and fry the slices of aubergine on both sides until they are an even brown on both sides. Put them into the bottom of a large pie dish or casserole and cover with the potato slices. Then spoon the cooked meat mixture on top, spreading it flat. Sprinkle with salt and pepper.

To make the savoury custard for the top: melt the butter in a saucepan and stir in the flour, then cook for half a minute. Take off the heat and add the bay leaf and the milk. Return to the heat and bring to the boil, stirring all the time. Mix the egg yolk with the cream. Take the sauce from the heat and allow to cool slightly. Then add most of the grated cheese and season well with salt and pepper. Stir in the egg yolk and cream mixture and pour the sauce over the top of the moussaka. Sprinkle on the rest of the cheese and the crumbs. Put the casserole into a moderate oven (160°C, 325°F, Gas Mark 3) and bake until the moussaka is very soft and the top browned – about 45 minutes–1 hour. Serve piping hot.

SERVES FOUR TO FIVE

VOL-AU-VENT

People very often muddle up the terms, vol-au-vent and bouchée. Strictly a bouchée is a mouthful-sized pastry case, made in the same shape and in the same way as a vol-au-vent. A vol-au-vent is either a one-portion pastry case about 7.5 cm/3 inches in diameter, or a large pastry case used for serving more than one person. Most vol-au-vent and bouchée fillings are savoury rather than sweet.

METRIC/IMPERIAL
225 g/8 oz puff pastry (see page 169 *or* use frozen)
flour for rolling
beaten egg

First set the oven. Puff pastry cooks best in a hot oven (230°C, 450°F, Gas Mark 8), but if making a very large vol-au-vent case it is better to cook it in a moderately hot oven (200°C, 400°F, Gas Mark 6).

To make a single large vol-au-vent: roll the pastry into a large round about 18 cm/7 inches in diameter and 1 cm/½ inch thick. Then use a tea plate or some other circular object about 15 cm/6 inches in diameter as a guide, and with a sharp knife cut round to give a perfect circle. It is important that the edge of the vol-au-vent should be cut with a knife, and not be the uncut edge of rolled pastry. Place the round of pastry on a wet baking tray and using a large pastry cutter, or a sharp knife, make a circular cut in the centre of the pastry, but not cutting right the way through. With the back of a knife mark a criss-cross pattern on the inner circle of the pastry top, and a different pattern (perhaps a star) on the outer circle (use the back of the knife, rather than the cutting side, because it is important to mark rather than cut into pastry). Beat the egg and use this to brush over the top of the pastry, taking care not to get any on the upright edge – this is likely to stick the layers together, preventing it from rising properly.

Bake in the oven for 30 minutes. The pastry should rise evenly and to a good height. Remove from the oven and using a sharp knife carefully cut out the centre circle. Put it aside for the moment, while you carefully spoon any uncooked pastry out of the centre of the pastry base with a teaspoon. Put the pastry case back into the oven for the inside to dry out, and if necessary put the pastry lid back too, upside down so that the underside dries out. After a minute or two take both lid and the pastry base out. The vol-au-vent is now ready for filling, but if not needed immediately can be stored, when stone cold, in an airtight tin. It should not be kept more than a few days.

To make the smaller, individual, vol-au-vent cases follow the same method, but cut the pastry into three circles about 7.5 cm/3 inches in diameter and 5 mm/¼ inch thick rather than into one large circle. Bouchée cases are 3.5 cm/1½ inches in diameter and the thickness of 2 mm/1⁄10 inch.

Individual vol-au-vents take about 20 minutes to bake and bouchée cases between 12 and 15 minutes, in a hot oven.

VOL-AU-VENT OF VEAL KIDNEY

METRIC/IMPERIAL
1 large vol-au-vent case (see above)
675 g/1½ lb veal kidney
50 g/2 oz butter
1 tablespoon flour
100 ml/4 fl oz Madeira
150 ml/¼ pint beef stock
lemon juice
salt and pepper
chopped parsley

Set the oven to moderate (160°C, 325°F, Gas Mark 3) and put the vol-au-vent case on a heatproof plate in the oven to reheat. Alternatively, time the cooking of the pastry case to coincide with the finished filling. The main thing is that the vol-au-vent case must be hot before the filling goes in.

Skin the veal kidney. Cut into 4–5 pieces. Melt the butter in a frying pan and when hot and foamy brown the pieces all over rapidly. Once they are brown turn the heat down, cover the pan and slowly cook for a further 10 minutes or so. Take the kidney out, slice fairly finely and keep warm.

Sprinkle the flour into the frying pan, scraping up any stuck bits on the bottom of the pan. Draw the pan off the heat again and stir in the Madeira and the stock. Bring slowly to the boil stirring all the time. Simmer for 4–5 minutes. Season with lemon juice, salt and pepper and add a good sprinkling of chopped parsley. Lastly add the kidneys with any blood that has run from them and bring up to boiling point. Do not cook any more but immediately fill the vol-au-vent case with the mixture.

NOTE One teaspoon of French mustard plus a little extra stock instead of the Madeira is a good variation.

SERVES FOUR

VOL-AU-VENT WITH SWEETBREAD AND CHICKEN FILLING

A vol-au-vent case can be filled with any savoury mixture. The following one is delicious.

METRIC/IMPERIAL
350 g/12 oz calf's or lamb's sweetbreads
40 g/1½ oz butter
1 onion, finely chopped
50 g/2 oz mushrooms, sliced
20 g/¾ oz flour
150 ml/¼ pint chicken stock
squeeze of lemon juice
225 g/8 oz chicken, cooked
salt and pepper
1 tablespoon cream

Put the sweetbreads into a bowl of cold water and soak them for 3 or 4 hours, changing the water every now and again (the water will become pink until all the blood from the sweetbreads has been extracted).

Now blanch the sweetbreads: put them into a saucepan, cover with cold water and bring very slowly to the boil. Barely simmer for 3 minutes, then drain and rinse under cold water. Dry well. Remove any remaining pink bits, blood vessels or membrane and chop roughly.

Melt the butter in a medium-sized saucepan and when foaming add the chopped onion and cook very gently until it is soft and transparent. Then add the sweetbreads and shake over a fairly fast heat for 2 minutes. Add the mushrooms and continue to cook for a further minute. Draw the pan off the heat and sprinkle in the flour. Stir this in until smooth and then add the chicken stock.

Return the pan to the heat and stir steadily while bringing up to the boil. Simmer for a minute or two, add the lemon juice and the pieces of cooked chicken. Taste for seasoning, adding salt and pepper if necessary. Add the cream last, stirring well, and then tip the mixture into the hot cooked vol-au-vent case. Serve at once.

SERVES FOUR

COQ AU VIN

*Coq au Vin has become such a cliché in small restaurants,
often made rather badly, that I hesitate to include
it. But a really good chicken cooked in red wine is
such a pleasure that I cannot resist it. The essential thing to
remember is that the wine you use should be good. It
should not necessarily be expensive but it is no good thinking
that wine that has turned to vinegar is 'good enough for cooking' – the
final dish will taste like chicken cooked in
vinegar. Also it is essential that the wine goes in right at the
beginning, with the stock, and is not added at the last
minute. Wine added to dishes which are then not given proper
cooking time gives a rather fermented and sour taste to the
dish, instead of the richness that it should impart.*

METRIC/IMPERIAL
4 rashers streaky bacon, with rind removed
50 g/2 oz butter
1 (1.5-kg/3½-lb) roasting chicken, jointed into 8 pieces
plain flour
225 g/8 oz button onions, peeled
225 g/8 oz button mushrooms
1 bay leaf
sprig of thyme
small bunch parsley
1 stick celery
1 small clove garlic, crushed
300 ml/½ pint good red wine
300 ml/½ pint chicken stock
salt and freshly ground black pepper
fried bread croûtons

In a large heavy saucepan cook the bacon, roughly chopped, until crisp. Using a perforated spoon lift the bacon on to a saucer. Add half the butter to the pan and wait until it is foaming. Dust each chicken joint with flour and then brown it in the hot butter, turning as necessary. It is most important that all the chicken joints are well browned on both sides. As they are done lift them out and keep them on a plate.

Add the rest of the butter to the pan and in it brown first the button onions, and then the mushrooms. At the end of the frying you should be left with very little butter in the pan, but if there is

127

more than a teaspoon tip it out. Tie the bay leaf, thyme, parsley (all except one sprig) and celery together with a piece of string. Now put everything (chicken, bacon bits, onions, mushrooms and bunch of herbs) into the saucepan, or into a clean casserole, and add the crushed garlic. Pour on the wine and the chicken stock and season well with salt and pepper. Cover tightly and simmer, either over a low heat, or in a moderate oven (180°C, 350°F, Gas Mark 4), until the chicken is tender, about 45 minutes–1 hour.

Lift out the bunch of herbs and re-dish the chicken in a clean casserole, or on a serving dish. If the sauce is too thin, or if it still tastes too 'winey', boil it rapidly to reduce it and then spoon over the chicken and vegetables. Chop the remaining sprig of parsley finely and use, with the fried croûtons, to garnish the dish at the last minute.

SERVES FOUR TO SIX

SPICY GRILLED CHICKEN

METRIC/IMPERIAL
2 tablespoons lemon juice
1 teaspoon paprika
½ teaspoon turmeric *or* 1 teaspoon curry powder
½ teaspoon English mustard
40 g/1½ oz butter
1 fresh chicken, jointed into 6 pieces
1 teaspoon sugar
salt and freshly ground black pepper

Heat the grill until blazing hot. Mix the lemon juice, paprika, turmeric, English mustard and butter together in a small saucepan over very gentle heat. Use this mixture to paint the chicken pieces well.

Grill the chicken, starting with the bony unattractive side and turning them over after 4 or 5 minutes to grill the skin side. As they grill keep basting them with the spicy, buttery mixture. When they are almost cooked (after about 14 minutes altogether), sprinkle them with sugar and return to the grill until the sugar caramelises to a crisp brown on top. Sprinkle with salt and plenty of freshly ground black pepper and serve as quickly as possible.

SERVES FOUR TO SIX

CHICKEN À LA MODE DE KIEV

Although the chicken has to be deep-fried at the last minute, and so is perhaps not the ideal party dish unless there is help at hand, it can be totally prepared for frying in advance, and the actual cooking takes only a few minutes. You need a well-ventilated kitchen, however!

METRIC/IMPERIAL
4 chicken breasts
100 g/4 oz butter
salt and pepper
1 tablespoon chopped parsley
juice of ½ lemon
seasoned flour
beaten egg
fresh white breadcrumbs
fat or oil for deep frying

Remove the bone and skin from each breast, and laying it flat on the table make a horizontal cut through the thick part of the flesh, but not slicing quite through, so that you can open it out like a book. Put each half-split open breast between two sheets of greaseproof paper or foil and gently but firmly flatten by tapping with a rolling pin or mallet. You should end up with thin chicken steaks, like veal escalopes.

Work the butter, salt, pepper and parsley together. Divide between the chicken pieces putting a spoonful in the centre, and sprinkle with lemon juice. Roll each breast up into a long parcel shape, pressing the joins together.

Roll first in flour, then in beaten egg, then in breadcrumbs. Chill very well. (If you have a freezer you can freeze them, well wrapped, at this stage. Thaw before cooking.)

Just before serving, heat the fat until a crumb will sizzle vigorously in it, then fry the chicken until golden and crisp – about 7 minutes. Because the now-melted butter trapped inside the parcel is likely to spurt when cut, the diner should cut a bite off the end first, not boldly stick a fork into the middle!

Restaurant chefs often leave the small wing bone attached to the breast, which sticks out of the end of the parcel making it look like a drumstick.

SERVES FOUR

Puddings

COEUR À LA CRÈME

*Coeur à la crème should be made in those old-
fashioned small heart-shaped moulds with holes in the bottom.
But, except in speciality cooks' shops or antique shops, one rarely sees
these today. This recipe describes an alternative method of producing
small individual sweet cheeses, but if one large mound of cheese will do,
simply put the cheese into a nylon sieve lined with muslin and leave to
drain overnight.*

METRIC/IMPERIAL
225 g/8 oz cottage cheese
300 ml/½ pint double cream
2 tablespoons castor sugar
2 egg whites
TO SERVE
300 ml/½ pint single cream

Make the sweet cheese two days before you want to eat it. Push the
cottage cheese through a sieve. Add the double cream to it and
flavour with castor sugar. Whisk the egg whites until stiff but not
dry and fold into the cheese mixture.

Spoon the mixture into individual ramekin dishes (it should fill
four good-sized ones) and secure a piece of muslin over the top of
each dish with a rubber band. Turn the ramekin dishes upside down
over a cake rack placed on a tray to catch the whey. Put into the
refrigerator overnight. To serve, turn each cheese (which will now
be fairly solidly set) on to a serving dish and pour over a spoon or two
of the single cream.

Coeur à la crème is sometimes served with fresh summer fruits,
such as grapes, strawberries or raspberries.

SERVES FOUR

BOODLE'S FOOL

METRIC/IMPERIAL
2 oranges
300 ml/½ pint double cream
about 2 tablespoons icing sugar

With a sharp knife or potato peeler pare half the rind of one of the oranges. It should have no white pith on the underside as this would be bitter. Cut the rind into tiny thin strips about 2.5 cm/1 inch long (needleshreds). Put these in a small pan of boiling water for 1 minute, rinse under cold water until cold then drain them.

Grate the rest of the orange rind finely and squeeze all the juice. Whip the cream until stiff enough to hold its shape, and then slowly beat in the orange juice, grated rind and sugar. Spoon the mixture into small glasses or individual china ramekin dishes, or into coffee cups (being very rich, each guest need only have very little).

Scatter the needleshreds of orange rind over the top to decorate.

SERVES FOUR

LEMON SYLLABUB

METRIC/IMPERIAL
2 large lemons
300 ml/½ pint double cream
about 2 tablespoons icing sugar
2 tablespoons dry white wine
1 large egg white *or* 2 small

Finely grate the rind of one of the lemons, and pare the peel of the other into very thin pieces. Make sure there is no pith on the peel as this can be bitter. Squeeze the juice from both the lemons.

Whip the cream until it is stiff enough to hold its shape and then slowly beat in the lemon juice, the grated rind and the icing sugar. Taste and add more icing sugar if necessary. Beat in the white wine and continue beating until the mixture will once more hold its shape.

Whisk the egg white or whites until stiff but by no means dry and carefully fold into the cream mixture.

Spoon into individual glasses and put in the refrigerator to chill.

Cut the lemon peel into tiny needleshreds and drop them into boiling water to cook for 1 minute. Scatter a few shreds on top of each syllabub. Chill well before serving.

SERVES FOUR

PAVLOVA

---

*Pavlova is the famous Australian meringue cake, not to be
confused with the French vacherin which is a crisp-all-through
meringue. Pavlova must be almost marshmallow-like
in the centre, rich and squashy.*

METRIC/IMPERIAL
2 egg whites
100 g/4 oz castor sugar
1 teaspoon cornflour
½ teaspoon vinegar
1 teaspoon vanilla essence
FOR THE FILLING
300 ml/½ pint double cream, whipped
fresh pineapple, walnuts, glacé cherries, or
any other fruit or nut combination

Set the oven to cool (140°C, 275°F, Gas Mark 1). Wrap a sheet of foil
over a baking tray, oil it lightly and dust with castor sugar.

Whisk the egg whites until stiff and dry, then add half the castor
sugar. Whisk again until the mixture is thick, shiny and very
smooth. It should hold its shape rigidly when you stop whisking.
Whisk in the cornflour, vinegar, vanilla essence and remaining
sugar. Using a spatula or the back of a large metal spoon spread the
meringue mixture in a flattish oval on the greased and sugared foil.
The meringue should be about 2.5 cm/1 inch all over, and need not
be higher at the sides than in the middle.

Bake in the oven for 50 minutes–1 hour. By this time the
meringue should be a very pale biscuit colour but still be squashy in
the middle. Take it from the oven and turn it over, upside down, on
the serving dish. Immediately peel off the paper while the meringue
is still hot (if you leave this job until the meringue gets cold you will
never get it off). The middle of the meringue will now sink slightly
giving a convenient hollow to fill with the whipped cream and the
fruit and nuts.

SERVES FOUR TO FIVE

BLACK JELLY WITH PORT

METRIC/IMPERIAL
450 g/1 lb fresh or frozen blackcurrants
225 g/8 oz granulated sugar
100 ml/4 fl oz port
1 heaped tablespoon powdered gelatine

Put the blackcurrants and the sugar into a heavy saucepan and heat together slowly, stirring occasionally with a wooden spoon. Once the juice has begun to run and the fruit is mushy push it through a sieve, extracting all the pips. Add the port to the blackcurrant purée and top up with enough water to make the mixture up to 600 ml/1 pint.

Put 3 tablespoons of water into a small heavy saucepan and sprinkle on the gelatine powder. Leave to soak for 10 minutes or so, and when 'spongy' warm over very gentle heat until the gelatine is clear and liquid. Stir into the blackcurrant mixture and mix well. Pour the jelly into a wet mould or bowl, and refrigerate until set.

To turn out, dip the mould into hot water just enough to loosen the sides of the jelly. Put a serving dish over the top and turn dish and mould over together, giving them both a sharp shake to dislodge the jelly. Serve with whipped cream or better still with egg custard (see page 79).   SERVES FOUR

CARAMEL TANGERINES

METRIC/IMPERIAL
225 g/8 oz granulated sugar
8 large or 20 small tangerines

Put half the sugar into a heavy-bottomed saucepan and heat gently until the sugar first melts and then caramelises. Do not stir during this process, but gently tilt the pan if necessary. When the toffee is brown, bubbly and clear gradually pour in 300 ml/½ pint of water (stand back as you do this: the caramel will splutter alarmingly). Now add the rest of the sugar and stir until the toffee lumps disappear and the sauce boils. Continue to boil until you have a slightly sticky syrup. Set aside to cool.

Peel the tangerines and put them in a glass dish. Spoon over the sauce, making sure that all the tangerines are coated. Chill well before serving.   SERVES SIX

CHOCOLATE LAYER CUP

Prepare the Chocolate Mousse and Ginger Syllabub mixtures according to the recipes on pages 139 and 140, but do not dish them up. In the bottom of four tall glasses place a layer of ginger syllabub. Spoon a layer of chocolate mousse on top. Continue the layers like this until all the mixtures are used, finishing with a layer of chocolate mousse. Refrigerate until set, preferably overnight.   SERVES FOUR

PRUNES IN PORT

This dish is deceptively mild-tasting. But unlike the nursery version of prunes and custard, too much of it can make you drunk!

METRIC/IMPERIAL
225 g/8 oz prunes (the squashy, quick-cooking kind)
about 300 ml/½ pint ruby port

Put the prunes, tightly packed, into a glass jar. Pour over the port to almost submerge the prunes. Leave for several days, or even for several weeks if in a cool place, until the prunes have plumped up and absorbed the port.

Serve with egg custard (see page 79).   SERVES FOUR

PINEAPPLE AND DATE SALAD

METRIC/IMPERIAL
1 large pineapple
100 g/4 oz best dates
icing sugar

Split the pineapple lengthways leaving half the leaves on each side of the pineapple. Using a grapefruit knife, carefully remove the flesh from the shells, without piercing the shells. Cut the flesh into bite-sized cubes, discarding any really woody bits from the core.

Cut the dates into thin slivers, discarding the stones. Combine the pineapple pieces and the dates in a bowl and sift over enough icing sugar to sweeten. Spoon the fruit salad back into the pineapple shells and chill well before serving plain or with vanilla ice cream.

SERVES FOUR TO FIVE

LEMON CUSTARD

METRIC/IMPERIAL
FOR THE CUSTARD
2 whole eggs
2 egg yolks
600 ml/1 pint creamy milk
25 g/1 oz sugar
finely grated rind of 2 small or 1 large lemon
FOR THE TOPPING
juice of the lemon or lemons
75 g/3 oz butter
225 g/8 oz granulated sugar
3 eggs
TO SERVE
whipped cream

Mix the custard ingredients together and strain into an ovenproof dish. Stand the dish in a roasting tin two-thirds full of hot water and bake in a moderate oven (160°C, 325°F, Gas Mark 3) until the custard has a good skin on top and is just set – about 40 minutes. Remove from the oven, and allow to cool to tepid.

Meanwhile make the lemon curd topping: put all the ingredients in a saucepan and stir briskly with a wooden spoon over moderate heat until thick. Spread on the lukewarm custard, and serve with the cream.   SERVES FOUR TO FIVE

GREEN SUMMER PEARS

METRIC/IMPERIAL
225 g/8 oz granulated sugar
600 ml/1 pint water
8 ripe pears
1 tablespoon lime juice cordial
1 tablespoon lemon juice
6 mint leaves
1 tablespoon crème de menthe

Put the sugar and the water in a large saucepan and bring slowly to the boil. Peel the pears, leaving on the stalks, and dunk them immediately in the syrup without allowing them time to discolour in the air. Poach the pears until they are tender right through. It is important that they should be thoroughly cooked (overcooking is better than not cooking enough) otherwise they may discolour in the middle.

When they are completely cooked, and almost glassy looking, carefully lift them out (use wooden spoons rather than metal ones, which tend to cut into the pear flesh) and put them into a glass serving dish. Add the lime juice cordial and the lemon juice to the syrup and 3 of the mint leaves. Boil the syrup rapidly for 4–5 minutes.

Allow the syrup to cool slightly and add the crème de menthe. Strain over the pears and chill thoroughly. When the syrup is stone cold add the 3 remaining mint leaves for decoration.

SERVES EIGHT

STRIPY FOOL

This is a very simple version of the fruit fool, made pretty enough for a party by the presentation. Any fruits can be used, or any combinations of fruits. A good one is greengage, rhubarb, plums and peaches. The following one is for all red fruit, though it is not necessary to use all four.

METRIC/IMPERIAL
225 g/8 oz cherries
225 g/8 oz blackcurrants
225 g/8 oz raspberries
225 g/8 oz strawberries
granulated sugar
600 ml/1 pint double cream

In four separate saucepans cook the fruits with sugar to taste. The cherries may need a tablespoon or so of water added to the pan, but the other fruits will need no water if the saucepans are put on a very gentle heat and the contents gently stirred with a wooden spoon. When the fruits are soft and pulpy push them through a nylon sieve into four separate bowls.

Whip the cream until it is just stiff enough to hold its shape. In individual glasses, or in a large glass serving dish, put first a layer of the cherry purée, then a layer of whipped cream, then the blackcurrant purée, then cream, then raspberry purée, then whipped cream, then strawberry purée, and finally more cream. It doesn't matter if the layers are not dead even. The dish will look very pretty anyway. Chill well before serving.   SERVES TEN

CHINA TEA FRUIT SALAD

*This is a fairly simple fruit salad, the only
exceptional thing about it being the addition of China tea to
the syrup. Any fruit can be used, but the following
combination is very good.*

METRIC/IMPERIAL
225 g/8 oz black grapes
225 g/8 oz honeydew melon
100 g/4 oz fresh strawberries
2 white pears
2 bananas
mint leaves (optional)
FOR THE SYRUP
175 g/6 oz granulated sugar
450 ml/¾ pint water
2 teaspoons China tea leaves

First prepare the syrup: put the sugar and the water on to boil
together, setting over a gentle heat at first so that the sugar dissolves
before the water boils. As soon as it is boiling well, pour it directly on
to the tea leaves in a bowl. Allow to get stone cold.

Meanwhile prepare all the fruit as you would for a fruit salad,
halving the grapes and taking the seeds from them, cutting the
melon into cubes, etc. Don't cut the fruit up too small – larger pieces
look better. Put the fruit into a pretty glass bowl and strain the cold
tea syrup over it. A few mint leaves can be added if liked.

SERVES FOUR

BANANA AND GRAPE VACHERIN

METRIC/IMPERIAL
3 egg whites
175 g/6 oz castor sugar
about 2 tablespoons lemon juice
1 banana
50 g/2 oz black grapes
50 g/2 oz green grapes
300 ml/½ pint double cream
25 g/1 oz dark chocolate

138

Set the oven to very cool (120°C, 250°F, Gas Mark ½). Lightly oil sheets of greaseproof paper or foil large enough to cover two big baking trays. Dust with castor sugar.

In a large bowl whisk the egg whites until stiff and rather dry. Add half the castor sugar and beat again until the meringue mixture looks shiny, and is very stiff. Carefully fold in the remaining castor sugar with a large metal spoon. Divide the mixture equally between the two baking trays and spread it into two flat rounds about the size of a dessert plate. Put the meringues in the oven to dry. This should take about 2½ hours. Halfway through the cooking time change the baking trays over, top to bottom and vice versa. The meringue is done when the paper will peel easily off the back. Cool on a wire rack.

Put the lemon juice in a bowl and slice the banana into it. Cut the grapes in half, and take out the seeds. (If you are really energetic the grapes can be peeled first: dip them into boiling water for a few seconds.) Whip the cream until it is just stiff enough to hold its shape. Combine half the cream with the grapes and the banana, and spread this mixture over one meringue round. Cover with the second meringue round and spread the rest of the cream on top of this, or pipe it into rosettes if you prefer. Grate the chocolate over the top and chill well before serving.

SERVES FOUR TO SIX

GINGER SYLLABUB

METRIC/IMPERIAL
4 tablespoons advocaat liqueur
2 heaped tablespoons ginger marmalade
300 ml/½ pint thick cream
1 or 2 pieces preserved ginger

Liquidise the advocaat and ginger marmalade together. Whip the cream stiffly and stir in the advocaat and ginger marmalade. Spoon into small glasses or little china pots or coffee cups. Decorate with two or three thin slivers of preserved ginger on top of each syllabub. Chill before serving.

SERVES FOUR

CHOCOLATE MOUSSE

METRIC/IMPERIAL
225 g/8 oz sweetened chocolate
150 ml/¼ pint water
1 tablespoon rum
40 g/1½ oz butter
4 eggs

Break up the chocolate and put it in a saucepan. Add the water. Heat, stirring, until it is smooth and has the consistency of thick cream. Cool slightly and stir in the rum and the butter.

Separate the eggs. Beat the yolks into the chocolate. Whisk the whites until stiff but not dry and fold into the mixture. Pour into individual pots, glasses or coffee cups. Refrigerate overnight.

The mousses may be decorated with whipped cream or chopped nuts, but classically they are served as they are. For a lighter, less rich mousse, leave out the egg yolks.

SERVES FOUR

HOT ORANGE PEARS WITH ORANGE SYRUP

METRIC/IMPERIAL
600 ml/1 pint water
150 g/5 oz castor sugar
6 pears, ripe but not overripe
3 oranges
juice of 1 lemon

Put the water and sugar together in a fairly deep narrow saucepan – just wide enough to take the pears side by side. Bring slowly to the boil, stirring until the sugar is dissolved. Peel the pears, leaving the stalks on. As each pear is peeled drop it into the boiling syrup. Allow the syrup to boil fast so that the bubbles completely cover the pears. This will prevent discolouring.

Finally pare the rind from the oranges, making sure that only the outer skin or zest is taken. Drop these strips of orange rind in with the cooking pears. Squeeze the juice of the oranges and put aside.

Boil the pears until they have a slightly glassy look. This can take anything up to an hour. Remove them carefully and put them into a serving dish. Then add the orange juice to the syrup in the saucepan and boil until it becomes fairly heavy – it should feel very sticky when felt with finger and thumb. Stir in the lemon juice. Scatter the orange peel over the pears and spoon over enough syrup to coat each pear well. Serve with whipped cream or ice cream.

SERVES FOUR TO SIX

CHINESE APPLE FRITTERS

This recipe is not really suitable for a party, unless it is held in the kitchen, or you know your friends so well that you can get up in the middle of the meal and start cooking. But the recipe is so delicious I could not resist its inclusion.

METRIC/IMPERIAL
1 tablespoon sesame seeds
4 dessert apples
cornflour
450 g/1 lb granulated sugar
½ tablespoon wine vinegar
oil for frying

Get everything ready at the beginning. The recipe itself is very simple, and the fritters are easy to make, but it is easy to get in a muddle as everything happens at the last minute.

You will need the oil in a deep fryer heated until a crumb will sizzle in it. On a plate or board safely away from the heat, you will need some absorbent paper to drain the apples on. Next to that you want a bowl filled with iced water, or water with a few cubes of ice floating in it. You also need a serving dish at the ready.

Brown the sesame seeds in the oven or in a dry frying pan. Peel the apples, core them and cut into large chunks. Toss in cornflour and put them ready in the frying basket, but not yet in the fat.

Put the sugar into a saucepan and add 250 ml/8 fl oz water. Heat very gently until the sugar has dissolved, then turn up the heat and let it bubble to an even toffee. When the sugar looks on the point of caramelising (when there is just a pale tinge of brown to it) pour in the vinegar, and let the sugar continue to bubble.

At this stage cook the apples. Plunge them into the deep fat and cook for about 4–5 minutes. Drain them on the absorbent paper as soon as they are soft. (They need not be brown, as long as they are crisp on the outside.)

Not so cheap . . .

Once the apples have been drained on the paper tip them into the caramel mixture, and turn them with a perforated metal spoon until they are well coated. Working as fast as you dare, lift each toffee apple out of the caramel, one by one, and while still in the spoon sprinkle quickly with the toasted sesame seeds, then drop into the icy water. Lift out of the water as soon as the caramel has hardened and cooled – about 20 seconds. Put them on to the serving dish and serve at once.

SERVES FOUR

DANISH APPLE CAKE

It is difficult to give exact quantities for this recipe, but it is extremely simple to make. The basic principle is to achieve layers of cooked sweetened apple, alternating with layers of crisply fried breadcrumbs, arranged in the form of a cake.

METRIC/IMPERIAL
about 75 g/3 oz butter
1 kg/2 lb apples, peeled and quartered
about 100 g/4 oz brown sugar
grated rind of 1 lemon
ground cinnamon
100 g/4 oz fresh white breadcrumbs
icing sugar
TO SERVE
egg custard (see page 79) *or* whipped cream

Heat a tablespoon of the butter in a frying pan and fry the apple pieces in it fairly briskly until they are beginning to soften, and looking a little brown. Tip them into an ovenproof dish of some sort. Then flavour them with the sugar, lemon rind and a sprinkling of cinnamon. Cook them in a slow oven until they are tender, but not broken up.

While they are cooking fry the breadcrumbs: melt some more of the butter and add the crumbs. They will quickly absorb the butter and should be moved and turned constantly during frying. Add the rest of the butter if the pan becomes too dry. When the crumbs are browned and crisp, remove them from the heat and immediately tip butter and crumbs on to a cold plate or into a cold bowl (if you leave them in the frying pan they will continue to brown).

Choose a serving plate with a good lip and in the bottom of it put a layer of cooked apple, patting it and pushing it into a solid shape, Then cover with half the crumbs, then a layer of apple, and finally another layer of crumbs. Sprinkle the top with icing sugar just before serving with whipped cream or egg custard.

If the apple cake is to be served cold it will set solidly, and can be cut in fairly neat slices. When hot it is more like a soft pudding.

NOTE Macaroon or biscuit crumbs may be added to the breadcrumbs if liked.

SERVES FOUR TO FIVE

FLAMING PEACHES

METRIC/IMPERIAL
6 large ripe peaches
50 g/2 oz butter
3 tablespoons sugar
juice of 1 large orange
3 tablespoons brandy
TO SERVE
whipped cream

Bring a saucepan of water to the boil and drop the peaches into it for five seconds or until the peel will come off them easily. Lift them out, peel them, cut them in half, and remove the stones.

Melt the butter in a large frying pan, or two small ones, and put the peach halves in, cut side down. Shake them over a moderately high heat until just beginning to brown. Turn all the peaches over, sprinkle in the sugar and continue to cook for a further 2 or 3 minutes. Add the orange juice, cover the pan or pans with a lid or foil and stew gently until the peaches are tender when pierced with a skewer. Remove the lid and boil the juices fast until reduced to a syrupy consistency. Pour in the brandy and set it alight, shaking the pan as the flames die down. Tip into a warm serving dish and serve hot or warm with cream handed separately.

NOTE For dramatic effect the peaches may be flamed in the dining room. If this is done the brandy should be warmed first in a small saucepan, set alight and poured, still flaming, over the peaches. They taste the same if flambéed in the kitchen, however!

SERVES FOUR

And
Simply
Extravagant

Starters

APPLES STUFFED WITH CRAB AND CELERY

METRIC/IMPERIAL
4 bright red perfect eating apples
2 tablespoons mayonnaise
2 tablespoons cream
juice and finely grated rind of ½ lemon
salt and pepper
1 (198-g/7-oz) can white king crab meat
1 stick celery, finely chopped
2 tablespoons salad oil
2 tablespoon wine vinegar

Wash the apples and polish them well with a soft tea towel. Slice off the narrower end (not the stalk end) about 1 cm/½ inch from the top of each apple. Using a teaspoon or melon baller, or grapefruit knife, scoop out the apple flesh from the large part of the apples. Discard the seeds and core and chip the rest of the flesh roughly. Mix it immediately with the mayonnaise and cream. Add the finely grated lemon rind, the juice and salt and pepper.

Carefully pick over the crab meat, removing any membrane or pieces of fine cartilage. Mix the crab meat into the apple mixture and add the chopped celery. Fill this mixture into the hollowed-out apples and replace the tops at a slightly jaunty angle.

Mix the oil and vinegar together and add salt and pepper. Spoon this over the apples to give them a shiny appearance. Chill before serving.

SERVES FOUR

And simply extravagant. . .

GUACAMOLE

This is a rich avocado pâté. It is sometimes filled into peeled hollowed-out tomatoes and eaten with a knife and fork rather than on toast.

METRIC/IMPERIAL
2 large ripe avocado pears, mashed
½ small onion, minced or finely chopped
juice of ½ small lemon
1 tablespoon olive oil
1 clove garlic, crushed
1 tablespoon tomato chutney *or* chopped fresh tomato
small pinch of ground coriander *or* 1 teaspoon
chopped fresh coriander leaves

Beat everything together and spoon into a serving bowl. Serve with hot toast.

SERVES FOUR

MELON WITH GINGER WINE

Ogen or Charentais melons are enormously expensive, and are so good on their own that gilding the lily is almost criminal. But should you be so lucky as to need a change from plain melon this is a good way to commit the crime.

Scoop the seeds from melon halves, small enough to give each person half a melon. Pour a tablespoon of ginger wine into each melon and chill thoroughly.

SMOKED SALMON PIE

METRIC/IMPERIAL

FOR THE PASTRY
275 g/10 oz plain flour
200 g/7 oz butter
1 teaspoon salt
2 egg yolks
2 tablespoons iced water

FOR THE FILLING
2 tablespoons grated Parmesan cheese
50 g/2 oz grated Gruyère cheese *or* strong Cheddar
2 large slices white bread, made into crumbs
75 g/3 oz butter
225 /8 oz smoked slamon, finely chopped
2 large sprigs fresh dill leaves *or* 2 teaspoons dill seeds
1 large clove garlic, crushed
2 (142-ml/5-fl oz) cartons soured cream
salt and freshly ground black pepper
lemon juice
beaten egg for glazing

First make the pastry. Sift the flour into a bowl. Make sure that the butter is soft but not sloppy. Use floured hands and a knife to cut the butter into tiny pieces and mix into the flour. Mix together in a teacup the salt, egg yolks, and 2 tablespoons icy water. Using first the knife and then one hand mix this into the flour and butter mixture, and lightly form into a soft dough. If the pastry is very sticky, chill well before using. Divide it into two pieces and roll each into a large rectangle. Put one rectangle on a Swiss roll tin and prick all over with a fork. Cover the other piece with a damp tea towel or piece of polythene to stop it drying out. Allow both pieces to 'rest' for 15 minutes, then bake the one on the Swiss roll tin in a moderately hot oven (190°C, 375°F, Gas Mark 5) for 15–20 minutes until it is a pale biscuit colour and just beginning to brown at the edges. Remove and allow it to cool.

Mix the cheeses and the breadcrumbs together. Melt the butter and stir this into the breadcrumb mixture. Scatter half of this all over the cooked pastry on the Swiss roll tin, leaving a good clear border all round the edge. Now sprinkle on top the smoked salmon and the dill, finely chopped. Crush the clove of garlic and sprinkle that on too and then spoon the soured cream all over the top. Grind black pepper on the filling, and season very lightly with salt. Sprinkle with

149

lemon juice and then scatter the remaining cheese and crumbs evenly all over the top. Cover the pie with the remaining piece of raw pastry, sticking the edges down with a little beaten egg. Pinch the edges with your fingers and thumb, or mark it with the prongs of a fork all round the border. Brush the top pastry with beaten egg, and decorate with pastry trimming if liked. Return the pie to the oven to bake the top crust, and to heat the filling. When the pie looks golden brown slide on to a serving tray to serve hot, or on to a wire rack if it is to be cooled.

SERVES EIGHT

STILTON SOUP

METRIC/IMPERIAL
50 g/2 oz butter
1 onion, finely chopped
2 sticks celery, sliced
40 g/1½ oz flour
3 tablespoons dry white wine
900 ml/1½ pints chicken or veal stock
300 ml/½ pint milk
100 g/4 oz Stilton cheese, grated or mashed
50 g/2oz strong Cheddar or Gruyère cheese, grated
4 tablespoons double cream
salt and pepper

Melt the butter in a heavy medium-sized saucepan and add the vegetables. Cook for 5 minutes then stir in the flour. Draw off the heat and stir in the wine and stock. Return to the heat and stir until boiling. Simmer the soup for 30 minutes or so, or until the wine has lost its harsh taste.

Now add the milk and the cheese and stir until just under boiling point. Push the soup through a sieve, or liquidise it in an electric blender.

Take care not to boil the soup when reheating it.

SERVES FOUR

LOBSTER BISQUE

Very good lobster bisque can be bought, admittedly expensively, in cans. It only needs doctoring with added cream and a dash of sherry. Fresh lobster bisque costs even more, but is satisfying to make.

METRIC/IMPERIAL
1 live lobster, weighing about 675 g/1½ lb
2 tablespoons oil
100 g/4 oz butter
1 medium onion, finely chopped
4 tablespoons brandy
juice of ½ lemon
1.15 litres/2 pints fish stock (made by boiling fish heads, skins, bones, etc. in water for 20 minutes, then straining)
1 bay leaf
small bunch of parsley
pinch of ground mace
40 g/1½ oz flour
3 tablespoons double cream
salt and white pepper
cayenne

Kill the lobster by pushing a sharp knife through its head (there is a cross on the shell, and you must pierce the middle of it). Split the lobster lengthways and remove the small stomach sac from the head and the nerve centre which is a thin dark thread running the length of the body. Discard these. Remove the coral, if there is any, and keep it. Remove the spongy lungs.

In a large frying pan heat the oil and a tablespoon or so of butter and put the lobster halves, flesh side down, into it. Fry like this for 5 minutes or so, then add the chopped onion, brandy and lemon juice. Cover with a piece of foil or a lid and put the whole frying pan into a moderate oven (180°C, 350°F, Gas Mark 4) for 15 minutes. Alternatively, continue to cook over very low heat on top of the cooker.

Pull out all the meat from the lobster, including the greenish creamy paste from the head. Keep the frying pan juices. Also keep the shells. In a saucepan put the fish stock (strained), the broken-up lobster shells (the more crushed the better), the bay leaf, the stalks from the parsley, and the ground mace. Simmer for 30 minutes or so. Now put all the lobster meat, another tablespoon or two of the butter and the coral (if any) into a mortar or an electric blender and beat to a smooth paste. Add the juices from the frying pan.

When the stock is ready (by now it should have taken some colour and flavour from the lobster shells) strain it into a jug. Rinse out the saucepan and in it melt the remaining butter (about 40 g/1½ oz). Stir in the flour and cook over a gentle heat until foaming. Then pour in the hot stock, draw the pan off the heat, and stir until smooth. Return the pan to the heat and stir until boiling. Add the creamed lobster and stir or whisk until smooth. Finally add the cream and reheat without boiling. Season to taste with salt, white pepper, and a good pinch of cayenne.

SERVES FOUR TO FIVE

HADDOCK SOUFFLÉ

Many a cook is nervous that a soufflé will become overcooked if the guests keep dinner waiting. A soufflé will sit perfectly happily in an oven for 10 minutes or so if the door is left open a crack and the oven is switched off.
This will slow down further cooking though, unfortunately, will not prevent it completely. The soufflé only starts to sink when brought out into the cold air, or when a cold serving spoon is plunged into it. But if the wait is likely to be longer than 10 minutes it is a good idea to have a sauce (perhaps a cheese sauce, or a lobster sauce — see following recipe) to serve with it. This will counteract any dryness.

METRIC/IMPERIAL
450 g/1 lb fresh haddock fillet, skinned
600 ml/1 pint creamy milk
1 onion, sliced
1 bay leaf
6 peppercorns
40 g/1½ oz butter
40 g/1½ oz plain flour
50 g/2 oz fresh white breadcrumbs
chopped parsley
1 teaspoon chopped fresh fennel (the herb, not the vegetable)
1 teaspoon anchovy essence
salt, pepper and paprika
5 whole eggs and 1 egg white

Butter two 15-cm/6-inch soufflé dishes, or one really large pie dish or cake tin. Set the oven to moderate (180°C, 350°F, Gas Mark 4).

Lay the fillets of fish in a roasting tin, cover them with their skins and pour on the milk. Add the onion, bay leaf and peppercorns. Cover with a piece of foil or greaseproof paper and bake in the oven for about 30 minutes, or until the fish feels firm to the touch and will flake easily. Take the fish from the oven, but don't turn it off. Strain the fishy milk into a jug, and keep the fish covered to prevent it drying out.

In a heavy saucepan melt the butter, add the flour and cook, stirring, over a gentle heat for 1 minute. Draw the pan off the heat and add all but 150 ml/¼ pint of the hot milk that the fish was cooked in. Stir steadily while bringing the sauce to the boil. Add the breadcrumbs to the remaining 150 ml/¼ pint of milk in the jug.

Flake the fish finely or blend it in an electric blender. Add the sauce to it with the chopped parsley, the chopped fennel, the breadcrumbs and the anchovy essence. Taste and add salt, pepper and paprika as necessary. Allow the mixture to cool slightly, then separate the eggs and add the yolks to the warm fish mixture. Whisk the egg whites until stiff but not dry and then fold them in too.

Turn the mixture immediately into the buttered soufflé dishes and with a knife cut through the mixture several times to break any over-large air pockets. Put in the middle of the oven to bake. After 30 minutes, but not before, open the oven door a crack and have a look. The soufflé should be well risen and when the dish is shaken gently the mixture should remain firm, not wobble alarmingly. Serve as soon as the soufflé is cooked.

SERVES FOUR TO SIX

CRAB OR LOBSTER SAUCE

METRIC/IMPERIAL
450 g/1 lb fish heads, bones and skin
300 ml/½ pint water
1 onion, sliced
handful of parsley stalks
25 g/1 oz butter
½ tablespoon flour
good pinch of paprika
1 (198-g/7-oz) can crab or lobster meat
1 tablespoon sherry
salt and pepper
150 ml/¼ pint single cream

Put the fish heads, bones and skin into a saucepan with the water, onion and parsley. Bring the water to the boil, and boil rapidly for 10 minutes or until the liquid is reduced to 150 ml/¼ pint.

Break up the crab or lobster meat with your fingers, removing any cartilage or membrane. In a small saucepan melt the butter and when it is foaming add the flour. Stir over a gentle heat for half a minute, then add the paprika and continue to cook for a few seconds more. Take the pan from the heat, add the reduced fish stock and stir well.

Return the sauce to the heat and stir until boiling. At this stage the sauce will be very thick. Beat the crab or lobster meat into it and add the sherry. Season with salt and pepper and lastly beat in the cream. Reheat carefully without boiling.

CHEESE SOUFFLÉ

METRIC/IMPERIAL
50 g/2 oz butter
50 g/2 oz flour
300 ml/½ pint milk
50 g/2 oz strong Cheddar cheese, grated, or Gruyère cheese, or a mixture of both
½ teaspoon made English mustard
salt and pepper
cayenne
4 eggs
grated Parmesan cheese

Set the oven to moderately hot (200°C, 400°F, Gas Mark 6). Brush a 15-cm/6-inch soufflé dish with melted butter.

Put the butter into a heavy-bottomed, medium-sized saucepan and melt it. Pour in the flour and add the milk. Stir over the heat while you bring the mixture to the boil. It will be a very thick paste and is ready when the mixture leaves the side of the pan as you stir it. Take it off the heat and allow to cool slightly.

Stir in the cheese and mustard, and season with salt, pepper and cayenne. Separate the eggs and beat the yolks into the mixture one at a time. In a large bowl whisk the egg whites until stiff but not dry, and beat a spoonful of them into the soufflé mixture. Then using a large metal spoon, carefully fold in the rest of the egg whites, taking care not to over-mix. Turn the mixture into the buttered soufflé dish, mixing any over-large pockets of egg white as you go. Lightly sprinkle with Parmesan cheese. Bake the soufflé for 30–40 minutes.

Of course ovens vary, and other factors (like the thickness of your soufflé dish) may affect the cooking time, but in any event do not look at the soufflé until it has been in the oven for 25 minutes. It is ready when the risen mixture remains fairly steady when the dish is given a slight shove. If it wobbles like a jelly it needs another 5 minutes or so.

Cheese soufflés are best served with a slightly runny middle which acts as a sauce to the crisper, drier outside. But if a completely cooked soufflé is wanted a warmed skewer, stuck into the risen sides of the soufflé, will come out clean. Do not remove the soufflé from the oven during testing. Serve at once.

SERVES FOUR

DEEP-FRIED CHEESE PUFFS

METRIC/IMPERIAL
95 g/3¾ oz flour
salt and pepper
cayenne
75 g/3 oz butter
225 ml/7½ fl oz water
50 g/2 oz strong Cheddar, grated
½ teaspoon made English mustard
3 eggs, lightly beaten
oil or fat for deep frying
grated Parmesan cheese
TO SERVE
tomato sauce (see page 45)

Sift the flour with the salt, pepper and cayenne into a large bowl. Put the butter and water into a heavy saucepan. Heat them, slowly at first, until the butter is completely melted. Then turn up the heat until the liquid is at a rolling boil. Immediately tip in the seasoned flour and beat vigorously with a wooden spoon. Draw the mixture off the heat and continue to beat until it is completely smooth and leaves the sides of the pan. Set aside to cool for 10 minutes.

Now gradually beat in the Cheddar cheese, mustard and the eggs (not all of them, you may not need so much). The mixture will go first slippery, then smooth and shiny. Continue adding small quantities of egg until you have a dropping consistency (this means that the mixture will fall off a spoon reluctantly, neither running off nor adhering obstinately).

And simply extravagant. . .

Heat the fat or oil in a deep fryer until a crumb will sizzle when dropped into it. Shape the mixture into small ping-pong balls and drop them into the hot fat. Do a few at a time, which will leave plenty of room for them to rise. Cook for 7–10 minutes or until they are puffy and golden. Lift them out and drain on absorbent paper. Dust with grated Parmesan cheese and serve at once, preferably with a thin tomato sauce.

SERVES FOUR TO SIX

OEUFS À LA VILLEROY

These eggs are a bit of a fiddle, but well worth doing if you have the time. They look mundanely like Scotch eggs, but when cut into, the liquid yolk should run richly over the mushroom coating and the crisp crust. They are fairly substantial so choose small eggs, and use as thin a coating of mushroom mixture as you can.

METRIC/IMPERIAL
50 g/2 oz butter
1 onion, finely chopped
350 g/12 oz mushrooms, finely chopped
50 g/2 oz flour
about 150 ml/¼ pint chicken stock
squeeze of lemon juice
salt and pepper
4 small eggs
seasoned flour
oil for deep frying
beaten egg
dry white breadcrumbs
sprigs of parsley

Melt the butter and add the onion. Cook over gentle heat until the onion is transparent and very soft. Then stir in the mushrooms and cook for a further minute or so. Then add the flour. Stir well and pour in *half* the stock, and a squeeze of lemon juice. Season with salt and pepper. Gradually bring the mixture to the boil, stirring vigorously all the time. It will become a thick heavy paste rather than a sauce. Add more stock if the mixture becomes impossibly thick – it should be just liquid. Allow to cool.

Prick the rounded end of the eggs with a needle to prevent them cracking and put them into boiling water. Cook them for 4 minutes

from the time the water reboils. Immediately plunge them into cold
water and allow to cool. Shell carefully – a tricky operation as they
are very delicate.

Flour a tray, board or working surface lightly with seasoned flour.
Divide the mushroom mixture (which will have set into a soft paste)
into 4 spoonfuls, putting them out on the floured surface. With a
floured hand squash the mixture into 4 flat cakes about the size of the
palm of your hand. Wrap each egg in one of these, carefully pressing
the edges together. The eggs must be completely covered.

Heat the oil in a deep fryer until it has a slight haze over it, and is
hot enough to make a crumb sizzle vigorously. Roll each egg in
beaten egg, and then in the breadcrumbs. Fry in the hot fat until
crisp and brown all over – about 2 minutes. When they are fried put
them on a warm serving dish and fry the parsley sprigs (which must
be absolutely dry) in the hot fat. As the parsley is dropped into the
fat it will sizzle and splutter alarmingly, but very quickly becomes a
brilliant green, and very crisp. Serve with the egg, as soon as you
can.

SERVES FOUR

BUCKWHEAT BLINIS

METRIC/IMPERIAL
225 g/8 oz buckwheat flour
½ teaspoon salt
25 g/1 oz fresh yeast *or* 15 g/½ oz dried yeast
1 heaped teaspoon sugar
750 ml/1¼ pint lukewarm milk
225 g/8 oz plain flour
3 eggs
oil for frying
TO SERVE
butter
soured cream
caviar, smoked salmon slices, or pickled herring
salt and freshly ground black pepper
lemon segments

In a large, warm mixing bowl mix the buckwheat flour with the salt.
In a jug cream the yeast with the sugar and add half the lukewarm
milk. Mix well and pour it into the buckwheat flour, stirring to a
paste. Cover the bowl with a sheet of oiled polythene or a floured tea

towel and leave in a warm place to rise.

Put the plain flour into another bowl and make a well in the centre. Into this drop 2 whole eggs and 1 egg yolk, keeping back a single egg white. Using a wooden spoon mix the eggs to a batter, bringing in the surrounding flour gradually, and adding the rest of the milk at the same time. When this batter is smooth, beat it into the yeasty one (which by now should have started to rise) and put the mixed batter, again covered with polythene, back in the warm place to rise again. Rising can take anything from 45 minutes–4 hours depending on the temperature of the warm place. A gentle rising, taking about 2 hours, is best.

Just before cooking, whip the remaining egg white until it will hold its shape, and then fold it into the batter. Lightly oil a very heavy frying pan and heat it. Pour enough of the batter into it to make a blini the size of a saucer. When the bubbles begin to rise, turn it over and cook the other side until brown too. The blinis should be fairly thick, more like large Scotch pancakes than French crêpes.

Serve the blinis hot with plenty of butter. Each guest spreads his blini liberally with butter, then with soured cream, then tops it with plenty of caviar, smoked salmon or herring. He may also add salt, freshly ground black pepper and a squeeze of lemon juice.

NOTE If blinis are to be made in advance they can be stored in the refrigerator, well wrapped. They can then be reheated by quickly frying again in butter, or they can be heated in the oven. Alternatively the batter mixture can be made, and once it has risen (but before the egg white is beaten into it) it can be refrigerated until needed. The coldness of the refrigerator will prevent further rising. The essential point about blinis is that they look mighty hearty, being large, but are fairly light. Most people will eat two of them for a starter and four for a main course. The guest must be encouraged to pile *plenty* of smoked salmon or whatever on top, and a really large tablespoon of soured cream. There is nothing worse than a mean blini!

SERVES SIX TO EIGHT

SALMON QUENELLES

Salmon is an amazingly expensive fish, but is very good. However, it hasn't got enought 'stickiness' to be used entirely on its own, and some whiting must be added to it.

METRIC/IMPERIAL
450 g/1 lb fresh salmon fillet
225 g/8 oz whiting fillet
4 white bread slices, without crusts
milk
2 egg whites
200 ml/7 fl oz double cream
salt and pepper
cayenne
FOR THE POACHING LIQUID
1.15 litres/2 pints water
150 ml/¼ pint vinegar
bunch of parsley
1 bay leaf
3 slices onion
fish heads, skins, bones, etc.
TO SERVE
1 (425-g/15-oz) can lobster bisque
150 ml/¼ pint single cream
2 teaspoons sherry
100 g/4 oz puff pastry

First make the pastry shapes. Roll out the pastry to the thickness of a large coin and cut it into crescent shapes with a fluted cutter. You need about 12 crescents. Bake these in a hot oven (220°C, 425°F, Gas Mark 7) until puffy and brown.

To make the poaching liquid simply combine all the ingredients and simmer them together for 25 minutes. Then strain the liquid into a clean shallow saucepan or deep frying pan.

Mince the salmon and the whiting twice on the finest mincer plate. Soak the bread in milk and squeeze it out. Put the fish and the soaked bread in an electric blender or into a mortar and pound or beat until thoroughly smooth. Whisk the egg whites in a small bowl until just frothy. Beat them into the fish bit by bit, allowing 2-minute intervals between each tablespoon or so. Season the mixture with salt, pepper, and a little cayenne. Leave in the refrigerator for a least 1 hour.

159

And simply extravagant. . .

Add the double cream, blending it in carefully, without too much beating. The mixture should feel firm and 'tacky'. It should not be over-sloppy or stodgy.

Using two wet dessertspoons, shape the fish mixture into egg-like blobs and drop them into the hot poaching liquid. They will take about 12 minutes to cook through, but the liquid must not be allowed to boil – it must barely simmer. When the quenelles feel firm to the touch lift them out with a perforated spoon, drain them on absorbent paper and put them into a serving dish.

Heat together the canned lobster bisque, the cream and the sherry and pour over the quenelles. Garnish with the hot pastry shapes. If liked, parsley leaves can be finely chopped and sprinkled over the quenelles.

SERVES FOUR TO SIX

RIVER TROUT WITH WATERCRESS SAUCE

METRIC/IMPERIAL
4 small rainbow trout
FOR THE POACHING LIQUID
600 ml/1 pint water
4 tablespoons vinegar
1 small carrot, sliced
2 or 3 slices onion
1 stick celery, sliced
6 peppercorns
1 bay leaf
1 tablespoon oil
½ teaspoon salt
FOR THE SAUCE
2 egg yolks
pinch of dry mustard
200 ml/7 fl oz salad oil
4 tablespoons olive oil
½ tablespoon vinegar
juice of ½ lemon
salt and pepper
4 tablespoons double cream
bunch of watercress
TO SERVE
2 or 3 sprigs of watercress   brown bread and butter

Put all the poaching liquid ingredients together into a saucepan and boil for 10 minutes. Allow to cool.

Lay the cleaned trout in a roasting tin and pour over the cold poaching liquid. Bake in a moderate oven (180°C, 350°F, Gas Mark 4) for about 30 minutes, until the trout feel firm to the touch and the eyes are white. Carefully lift the fish from the liquid and put them on a board, lightly covered with foil or plastic wrap to prevent them drying out (they can be cooled in the liquid in which they were cooked but the roasting tin should then be stood in a sink of cold water so that it cools rapidly and prevents the fish overcooking).

While the fish is cooling make the sauce. Whizz the egg yolks and mustard in an electric blender or beat the egg yolks with the mustard in a bowl. Gradually add the two oils, drip by drip at first, whisking or beating all the time. As the emulsion thickens the oil can be added with less caution. When you have added all the oil, add the lemon juice, salt and pepper, and the double cream. If the mayonnaise is stodgily thick, thin it with a little water or milk.

Dip the watercress into boiling water for 2–3 seconds, until it is limp and very bright green. Drain it, rinse in cold water to set the colour, and chop and mash to a fine paste. Add to the mayonnaise. If you have a blender the sauce can be whizzed with the watercress leaves.

Carefully remove the skin from the trout, but leaving on the tails and heads if you like. Coat the fish carefully with the green sauce just before serving. Use sprigs of watercress to decorate, and serve with brown bread and butter.

SERVES FOUR

Main Courses

SALMON EN CROÛTE

METRIC/IMPERIAL
1 (1.75-kg/4-lb) salmon or sea trout
450 g/1 lb puff pastry
(see page 169 *or* use frozen)
semolina
lemon juice
butter
salt and freshly ground black pepper
2 or 3 sprigs of tarragon
1 egg, beaten
FOR THE SAUCE
50 g/2 oz butter
20 g/¾ oz flour
3 tablespoons white wine
300 ml/½ pint fish stock
salt and white pepper
1 teaspoon chopped fresh tarragon or parsley
2 tablespoons double cream
FOR THE STOCK
2 slices onion
1 bay leaf
small handful of parsley
1 teaspoon peppercorns
salt
bones, skin and head from the salmon
600 ml/1 pint water

Fillet the fish, keeping the 4 fillets as intact as possible. Skin the
fillets and put the skin, bones, head and fins into a saucepan with the
other stock ingredients. Bring up to the boil and simmer for 30
minutes. Then strain into a measuring jug and throw away the
bones, etc. Heat the oven to hot (230°C, 450°F, Gas Mark 8).

Roll out a third of the pastry into a long thin piece, cutting it roughly the shape of the original salmon. Prick it all over and bake it for 20 minutes or until crisp. Turn it over halfway through the cooking time to cook both sides evenly. Take it out and allow to cool. Cool the baking tray too, then put the pastry back on it.

Sprinkle the pastry evenly with semolina (this will absorb some of the cooking juices of the fish, and prevent the bottom layer of pastry becoming soggy). Lay 2 of the fish fillets on the pastry and sprinkle them with a little lemon juice and spread with butter. Add salt, plenty of freshly ground black pepper and a few tarragon leaves, either chopped or whole, then lay the other 2 fillets on top, and again add seasoning, tarragon and butter.

Roll the rest of the pastry out into a large sheet big enough to easily cover both cooked pastry and fish. Lay it over the top, taking care not to pull or stretch it. Trim it to shape, leaving a 2.5-cm/1-inch margin all the way round. Using a fish slice, gently lift the cooked pastry and fish and tuck the edges of the raw pastry under, trimming excess pieces off. Using a pastry cutter, the end of a teaspoon, or the nozzle of a plain forcing bag pipe, mark the fish from the head to the tail with scales. You need to press quite deeply into the pastry, but avoiding cutting right through. Give the fish a pastry eye, and cut fine strips of pastry to represent the gills and tail fin. Brush the whole fish with the beaten egg and return it to the oven for 15 minutes to brown and puff up the pastry. Then lower the oven to moderate (160°C, 325°F, Gas Mark 3), and cook for a further 20 minutes. The fish can be tested to see whether or not it is cooked by pushing a sharp skewer through the pastry into the fish. There should be no resistance (other than that of the pastry) at all. If the fish fillets still feel resistant they are not yet cooked.

While the fish is cooking make the sauce: melt half the butter in a saucepan, add the flour and stir over the heat for half a minute or until the butter is foaming. Draw off the heat and add the wine and the stock. Stir until well blended, then return to the heat and stir until boiling and thickened. Reduce the heat and simmer for 30 minutes or so. Taste and add salt, pepper, and the chopped tarragon or parsley. Draw off the heat and beat in the remaining butter. Lastly add the cream. When the fish is cooked take it to the table whole to give everybody a chance to admire it, then split it right down the middle and pour in the sauce. Or pour in some of the sauce and hand the rest separately.

SERVES EIGHT

TURBOT STUFFED WITH LOBSTER AND SCALLOP MOUSSE AND SERVED WITH SCALLOP CREAM SAUCE

This recipe, a sort of heavenly fish parcel, is expensive and difficult to make but satisfying to achieve, and oh me, oh my, it is delicious. For really keen cooks only!

METRIC/IMPERIAL

1 (1.5-kg/3-lb) live lobster
4 fillets sole, plus the skin, bones and head
16 flat thin slices (about the size of the palm of your hand)
of turbot *or* brill
few slices onion
1 bay leaf
salt and pepper
600 ml/1 pint water
100 g/4 oz dried morels (mushroom-like fungi from France)
3 tablespoons finely chopped shallots
15 g/½ oz butter
little crushed garlic
flour
Chablis *or* similar white wine
Armagnac *or* brandy
2 teaspoons tomato purée
1 tablespoon chopped fresh tarragon

FOR THE MOUSSE

16 fresh scallops in their shells
1 egg white
150 ml/¼ pint double cream
salt and pepper
Armagnac *or* brandy

FOR THE SAUCE

100 g/4 oz shallots, finely chopped
150 ml/¼ pint Chablis or other white wine
150 ml/¼ pint dry Vermouth
450 ml/¾ pint double cream
cayenne

TO SERVE

450 g/1 lb fresh spinach
butter
puff pastry crescents to garnish (optional)

Ask the fishmonger to kill the lobster for you, to split it and remove the stomach sac and intestine. Pull out the flesh from the tail shell and keep it raw for the mousse. Put the head, claws, legs and shell into a small saucepan and set aside in a cool place while you make the fish stock.

Put the bones, skin and head of the sole and any turbot or brill trimmings or bones into a saucepan with the sliced onion, bay leaf, salt, pepper and water. Simmer for 15 minutes, then strain and allow to cool. When quite cold, pour over the lobster head, claws, etc. and poach gently until the lobster is cooked – about 12 minutes. Take the flesh from the claws and head (including the greyish creamy part), and from the legs, and chop it up. Crush the shells and return to the stock pan to simmer for a further 10 minutes.

Soak the dried morels in several changes of water until soft. Cut them up. In a small heavy saucepan gently cook the chopped shallots in the butter until soft and transparent. Add the morels and the merest suspicion of crushed garlic. Allow to simmer for 1 minute, then add a heaped teaspoon of flour, stir well and add 2 tablespoons of Chablis, a dash of Armagnac and the tomato purée. Stir over heat, adding enough fish stock to give a sauce of creamy consistency. Add the cooked lobster meat, the chopped fresh tarragon, and salt and pepper to taste. Set the mixture aside.

To make the mousse: take the raw lobster and the fillets of sole, and pound them together (or mix in an electric blender until quite smooth). Then lift the scallops from their shells (keeping the shells) and remove the orange/pink corals, which you must set aside for the sauce. Remove and discard the muscle (found opposite the coral) from each scallop. Pound the scallop flesh with the lobster and sole. Then beat in the egg white and the double cream and season with salt, pepper and a dash of Armagnac.

To make the sauce: gently cook the chopped shallots in the white wine and the Vermouth until soft. Add 150 ml/¼ pint of the fish stock and simmer for 5 minutes. Then stir in the double cream. Season with cayenne. Set the sauce aside while you prepare the scallop corals.

Strain the remaining fish stock from the lobster shells and boil it rapidly until you are left with a tablespoon or so of thick, clearish liquid. This is concentrated 'glace de poisson'. Add the scallop corals to it, simmer for 1 minute, then pound stock and corals together to make a smooth pink creamy paste. Set aside – you will add it to the sauce at the last minute.

Now, having prepared your lobster and morel mixture, your lobster and scallop mousse and your sauce, you are ready to start on the main construction!

Wash the spinach leaves, remove any tough stalks and plunge them into a little boiling water for a few seconds only. Drain them immediately and dunk into cold water to set the bright green colour.

Take the 8 deeper scallop shells, wash them and butter them well. Line each shell with a fillet of turbot or brill. Follow this with a layer of the spinach and then a layer of mousse. Into the centre of this put a spoonful of the morel, lobster and tarragon-flavoured mixture. Then another layer of lobster mousse, another of spinach and cover with the remaining fish fillets.

Brush the top with melted butter. Put the 8 filled scallop dishes into a roasting tin and pour in boiling water, round the shells, to cover the tin to a depth of 5 mm/¼ inch. Cover the whole dish with foil and bake in a moderate oven (180°C, 350°F, Gas Mark 4) for 20 minutes.

While they are cooking, reheat the sauce and add the scallop coral paste. When you are ready to go, slide each little parcel out of its scallop shell, turn it over on to a serving platter and pour over the hot sauce.

And if that is not enough you could add a few puff pastry crescents to add a crisp contrast to the delicious creamy texture of the dish!

SERVES EIGHT

JAMBALAYA

METRIC/IMPERIAL
olive oil for frying
225 g/8 oz lean pork, cut into cubes
1 frankfurter sausage, sliced
5–7.5 cm/2–3 inches garlic sausage, peeled and cut into cubes
1 onion, finely chopped
1 stick celery, finely chopped
225 g/8 oz peeled prawns, cooked or raw
100 g/4 oz long-grain rice
½ teaspoon ground ginger
¼ teaspoon paprika
¼ teaspoon turmeric
salt and freshly ground black pepper
lemon juice
about 300 ml/½ pint chicken stock

Heat 2–3 tablespoons oil in a heavy, wide saucepan and in it fry the pieces of pork fairly fast until evenly browned all over. With a perforated spoon lift them out and set aside. Next fry the frankfurter and the garlic sausage in the same way. Turn the heat down a little and fry the onion and celery until somewhat softened, and just turning colour. Add them to the fried pork and sausages. Next put in the prawns and toss them in the hot oil (adding a little more if necessary) until hot and cooked, but do not try to brown them. Lift them out too.

Finally fry the rice: turn the heat up, tip in the rice, and shake and stir over fairly high heat until the rice is opaque, and beginning to brown. Turn down the heat and put back all the fried ingredients. Add the spices, salt and pepper, squeeze of lemon and the chicken stock. Simmer gently until the stock is absorbed and the rice is cooked. This should take 20–25 minutes.

SERVES FOUR

STEAK TARTARE

Fillet is the classic steak for this dish but costs a fortune. Rump is excellent, and skirt will do very well. It seems that almost anything else can go into a steak tartare according to the likes of the diner. All the ingredients listed with 'optional' after them are the ones I disapprove of, but which many people insist on. Make the basic steak tartare as I have indicated and if you feel it needs something sharper, experiment with any of the other ingredients. I think it is delicious as it is.

METRIC/IMPERIAL
450 g/1 lb good lean steak
3 egg yolks
5 tablespoons salad oil
1 tablespoon finely chopped parsley
50 g/2 oz onion, finely chopped
salt and freshly ground black pepper
Worcestershire sauce (optional)
finely chopped green pepper (optional)
finely chopped capers (optional)
finely chopped gherkins (optional)
thin slivers of anchovy fillets (optional)

Simply mince or chop the steak very finely and add everthing else, starting with the yolks and oil and then adding the flavourings. Shape into 4 patties and serve with crisp lettuce leaves.

NOTE It is a great joke among waiters that ignorant customers, not realising that steak tartare is served raw, order it 'medium rare with chips', but I think that at least the chips are a good idea! In fact any hot potato goes well with the cold steak, especially new potatoes boiled with mint, baked potatoes cooked in their jackets and, of course, chips.

SERVES FOUR

PUFF PASTRY

If this is your first go at puff pastry use 150 g/5 oz rather than 200 g/7 oz of butter. It will still be delicious and a little easier to handle. The secret of success is to chill the pastry for 15 minutes or more in the refrigerator as soon as the butter looks in danger of coming through the pastry. So resist the temptation to keep going, with the pastry getting warmer and stickier every minute. Also, have the block of butter firm and cool when you start, but not rock hard.

METRIC/IMPERIAL
225 g/8 oz plain flour
salt
25 g/1 oz lard
150–200 g/5–7 oz butter or margarine
150 ml/¼ pint water

Sift the flour with the salt and rub in the lard. Mix the water into it and knead to a soft dough. Leave wrapped in a cool place for 20 minutes.

On a floured surface, roll out to 13 by 25 cm/5 by 10 inches. Using a floured rolling pin, tap the block of butter until it is flattened to about 1.5 cm/¾ inch deep, like a cake of soap. Put it in the middle of the pastry and fold both ends over it to wrap it up. Press the sides together to seal them. Now tap the pastry parcel with the rolling pin to flatten it slightly. Then roll out, until the pastry is three times as long as it is wide. Fold it evenly in three and press the edges together to seal them. Give the block a half turn (90°) clockwise, and again roll out into a long strip. Again fold in three.

Repeat this rolling, folding and turning procedure until the pastry no longer looks streaky (six times should be about right, but unless you are lucky you will need to relax and rest the pastry in a cool place between rollings).

And simply extravagant. . .

FILLET OF BEEF IN PASTRY

*With the price of beef fillet so high this recipe is fast becoming a folk
memory. But should you get fillet by some happy chance this is probably
the best way of serving it. The pastry encloses the meat, trapping the
flavour and juices, and the pastry itself is so delicious that the dish is
'stretched' to serve more people than a plain whole roasted fillet without
pastry would do.*

METRIC/IMPERIAL
1.75-kg/4-lb piece of beef fillet cut from the thick end, and trimmed
of all membrane and fat
50 g/2oz butter
1 onion, chopped
1 clove garlic, crushed
225 g/8 oz flat black mushrooms, sliced
salt and pepper
little French mustard
225 g/8 oz puff pastry
(see page 169 *or* use frozen)
1 egg, beaten

Brown the fillet in a hot oven (230°C, 450°F, Gas Mark 8) for 30
minutes. It will still be rare inside, but the outside will be sealed and
brown. Take it out and allow to cool on a plate.

In a large saucepan melt the butter and in it cook the onion. When
it is transparent and soft add the garlic and cook for a further half a
minute. Then add the sliced mushrooms and cook them too. After
5–6 minutes you should have a good mushy mixture. Add salt and
pepper and then allow to get stone cold.

Take a third of the pastry and roll it into a rectangle roughly the
size and shape of the beef fillet. Prick it all over and cook it in the hot
oven until crisp – about 12 minutes. Turn it over and return to the
oven to cook the other side for a further 4–5 minutes. Take it out and
allow to cool.

Spread the beef fillet very thinly with mustard. Add any blood
that has run from the beef to the mushroom and onion mixture. Put
the cooled pastry on a cold baking tray and put the beef on top of it.
Spoon the mushroom mixture over the beef as neatly as you can.
Roll the remaining pastry out into a thin sheet large enough to amply
cover the beef and pastry.

Carefully lay it over the top, taking care not to pull it or stretch it.
Cut round the edges so that you have a margin of about 2.5 cm/1 inch

all round the bottom layer of pastry. Tuck this margin under the pastry, using a fish slice to help you lift it. Trim any excess pastry from the corners and keep it for decoration. Brush the pastry all over with beaten egg. Make pastry leaves or other shapes with the pastry trimmings and arrange them on the top of the fillet. Brush again with beaten egg.

Twenty minutes before the beef is due to be eaten return it to the oven to cook the pastry. If it is not brown and crisp after 20 minutes, give it another 5 minutes.

Serve immediately and carve at the table. (Carving it in advance will produce a grey and unappetising result.)

NOTE This recipe assumes that rare beef is required. If medium beef is wanted the preliminary cooking time (of the beef, without the pastry) should be increased to 40 minutes, and if well-done beef is required it should be cooked for 50 minutes in the first place.

SERVES EIGHT

LARDED LEG OF LAMB WITH CELERIAC

This recipe is quite time-consuming to do, but the result is truly wonderful. The larding bacon, or pork fat which is sometimes used, must be tough enough to be cut into thin strips and threaded with a needle through meat. Obviously soft lard is no good. The fat from the back or belly of the pig is generally used.

METRIC/IMPERIAL
1.5-kg/3-lb leg of lamb
50 g/2 oz larding bacon, cut into thin strips
salt and freshly ground black pepper
1 clove garlic, peeled and cut into thin slivers
sprig of rosemary
7g/¼ oz lamb dripping *or* 15 g/½ oz butter
8 artichoke bottoms *or* 8 globe artichokes
225 g/8 oz celeriac
100 g/4 oz mashed potato
25 g/1 oz butter
FOR THE GRAVY
2 teaspoons flour
150 ml/¼ pint stock

Set the oven to moderate (180°C, 350°F, Gas Mark 4). With a larding needle, thread bacon strips or pork fat strips into the lamb flesh evenly throughout the meat. Season the lamb all over with salt and freshly ground black pepper, and stick the slivers of garlic into the meat near the bone. Sprinkle with rosemary leaves and smear with a little butter. Heat the dripping or butter in the roasting tin and add the lamb. Roast, basting frequently, for 2 hours (or 25 minutes per half kilo/per lb). When the lamb is done, the meat should still be faintly pink inside, but if you prefer the lamb well done cook until the juices run clear from the meat when it is pierced with a skewer.

Wash the artichokes (if using fresh ones) and cook them in salt water for 30 minutes or so until done. They are ready when a leaf can be pulled out with ease. Meanwhile, boil the peeled celeriac in salted water until tender, drain it and mash well. Put the celeriac through a vegetable mouli or into an electric blender to get it free of stringiness. Then beat in the mashed potato, half the butter, and season well with salt and pepper.

When the artichokes are cooked, peel away all the leaves (do not throw them away – serve them as a starter with vinaigrette, or use them to flavour soup). Using a teaspoon scrape out all the prickly choke so that you are left with just the artichoke bottoms. (If using canned artichoke bottoms none of the cooking and preparing instructions apply, of course.) Stuff the artichoke bottoms with the potato and celeriac mixture and brush them with a little melted butter.

When the lamb is cooked take it from the oven and put it on a warmed serving dish. Surround it with the stuffed artichokes and keep warm. Pour all but a tablespoon or so of fat from the juices in the roasting tin. Whisk the flour into the tin, whisking out any lumps. Add the stock and stir until boiling. If the sauce is too thick, add a little more stock or water. Taste and season as necessary. Strain into a warmed gravy boat and serve with the lamb.

SERVES FOUR TO SIX

LAMB WITH DILL SAUCE

METRIC/IMPERIAL
1 kg/2 lb lean leg of lamb, cut into large chunks
1 onion, sliced
1 carrot, sliced
2 teaspoons crushed dill seeds *or* 3 or 4 sprigs of fresh dill
1 bay leaf
12 peppercorns
about 750 ml/1¼ pints chicken stock *or*
1 chicken stock cube and water
FOR THE SAUCE
1 tablespoon flour
25 g/1 oz butter
1 egg yolk
3 tablespoons double cream
2 teaspoons lemon juice
salt and pepper

Put the meat, onion, carrot, seeds or stalks of dill (but not the fresh leaves), bay leaf, peppercorns, stock cube, if used, into a saucepan. Cover with the stock or water and bring slowly to the boil. Turn down the heat and cook as slowly as possible for about an hour, or until the meat is tender.

Lift out the cubes of meat, discarding the bay leaf and dill stalks, and put them into a casserole or serving dish. Cover to prevent drying out, and keep warm. Strain the stock, and skim off all the fat. An easy way to do this is to lay successive sheets of absorbent kitchen paper on the top of the liquid to soak up the fat. When quite fat-free, measure the remaining liquid, making it up with water if necessary to 450 ml/¾ pint, or reducing it by boiling rapidly. Return it to the saucepan.

Mix the butter and flour together into a smooth paste. Whisk this into the hot stock, continuing to whisk steadily until the sauce is smooth. Bring to the boil and simmer for 2 minutes. Mix the egg yolk and cream in a bowl. Stir a little of the hot sauce into the cream mixture, and then stir this back into the sauce, taking care not to boil the sauce now or the yolk will scramble. Flavour the sauce with the lemon juice and add more salt and pepper if necessary. Chop the dill leaves if you have them, and stir them in. Pour over the meat and serve at once.

SERVES SIX

And simply extravagant. . .

ROAST LEG OF LAMB WITH FLAGEOLETS

METRIC/IMPERIAL
1.75-kg/4-lb leg of lamb, boned
salt and pepper
sprig of rosemary
butter
1 onion, sliced
1 clove garlic, crushed
1 (500-g/18-oz) can flageolet beans
4 or 5 lettuce leaves, shredded

Set the oven to moderately hot (200°C, 400°F, Gas Mark 6). Season the lamb inside and out with salt and pepper and sprinkle over the rosemary leaves. Melt a tablespoon or so of butter in a roasting tin and put in the lamb. Baste with the melted butter and roast for 1½ hours.

Meanwhile, melt about a tablespoon of butter in a large frying pan or heavy saucepan and in it cook the sliced onion until it is soft and transparent. Add the crushed garlic and cook for a further minute.

Drain the flageolet beans and rinse them under plenty of running water to remove the starchy liquid. Just before serving add the shredded lettuce to the onion and garlic in the pan and mix well. Cook for half a minute and then add the flageolet beans. Cover with a lid and allow the beans to heat without too much stirring. Serve the roast lamb surrounded by the flageolets.

If gravy is wanted it can be made in the traditional way with the juices in the bottom of the roasting tin.

GUARD OF HONOUR

This is a simple roast lamb recipe, but the racks are arranged attractively. Small paper cutlet frills are traditionally put on the ends of the cutlet bones making the dish look festive and professional. But they aren't necessary.

METRIC/IMPERIAL
2 best end neck of lamb, each with 7 cutlets, chined
1 tablespoon melted butter
sprig of rosemary
salt and pepper

Have the butcher trim the cutlet bones back so that they are only about 5 cm/2 inches long. Scrape the skin and meat from the ends leaving 2.5 cm/1 inch of each bone clear. Stand the two best end of neck in a roasting tin with their bones interlocking at the top and the heavy part of the meat at the bottom, forming an arch. Brush well with melted butter and sprinkle all over with rosemary leaves and salt and pepper.

Roast the lamb (220°C, 425°F, Gas Mark 7) for 1 hour (for pink lamb) or 1¼ hours (for better done lamb). Baste the meat with the butter and juices in the tin two or three times during cooking. Also, if the bones look in danger of browning too much or burning, wrap them in wet greaseproof paper held in place with a layer of foil.

Dish the guard of honour on a warm platter and put the cutlet frills in place if you have them. Place a bunch of watercress at the side.

SERVES SIX TO EIGHT

ROAST RACK OF LAMB WITH MUSTARD AND HERBS

METRIC/IMPERIAL
1 7-bone rack of best end of lamb,
chined and skinned
1 teaspoon made English mustard
2 tablespoons fresh white breadcrumbs
2 tablespoons finely chopped mixed herbs
(mint, chives, parsley, chervil, thyme and a little rosemary are good)
salt and freshly ground black pepper
½ tablespoon softened butter

Cut the cutlet bones back so that they are only 3.5 cm/1½ inches long. Scrape the meat away from the ends of them so that about 2.5 cm/1 inch of each bone is exposed.

Mix the mustard, breadcrumbs, herbs, salt and pepper and butter together. Spread this mixture all over the rounded skinned side of the best end.

Roast the meat, round side up, in a hot oven (220°C, 425°F, Gas Mark 7) for 1 hour. This will give a distinctly underdone lamb. If you like it well done cook it for a further 15 minutes. Before serving spoon any butter or juices that have run from the meat over the top.

SERVES THREE TO FOUR

LAMB STEAKS WITH
GARLIC AND ROSEMARY

Preparation must begin at least three days in advance.

METRIC/IMPERIAL
2 cloves garlic, crushed
4 lamb steaks, each weighing about 225 g/8 oz, cut from the leg
4 tablespoons salad oil
2 sprigs of rosemary, chopped
salt and freshly ground black pepper

Rub the garlic all over the lamb steaks. Lay them in a dish and spoon over the oil. Cover with a piece of polythene wrap (this is to prevent the garlic smell getting into other food in the fridge) and refrigerate for three days.

Twenty minutes before serving, heat the grill until blazing hot, or heat a frying pan until really hot. Wipe most of the oil and garlic off the steaks and sprinkle with the chopped rosemary and with plenty of freshly ground black pepper, but not with salt. Grill or fry the steaks as fast as you dare until brown on both sides and barely pink in the middle. Add a sprinkling of salt just before serving, and pour the pan or grill juices over the steaks.

SERVES FOUR

HUNGARIAN VEAL STEAKS

METRIC/IMPERIAL
4 good thick slices aubergine
675 g/1½ lb boneless veal, sirloin or fillet
225 g/8 oz larding pork fat *or* thin rind streaky bacon rashers
about 50 g/2 oz butter
about 25 g/1 oz flour, well seasoned
2 tablespoons cooking oil
1 shallot or small onion, finely chopped
1 teaspoon paprika
3 tablespoons white wine
150 ml/¼ pint single cream
salt and pepper
FOR THE MORNAY SAUCE
300 ml/½ pint milk
2–3 slices onion
1 bay leaf
1–2 sprigs of parsley
salt and pepper
20 g/¾ oz butter
20 g/¾ oz flour
pinch of dry English mustard
65 g/2½ oz strong Cheddar cheese, grated

Begin with the Mornay sauce. Put the milk, onion, bay leaf, parsley and salt and pepper into a saucepan and bring slowly to the boil. In a second saucepan melt the butter and stir in the flour. Cook for half a minute or until the butter is foamy. Draw off the heat and stir in the English mustard, and then strain on the hot flavoured milk. Blend well, return to the heat and stir until boiling. Whisk with a wire whisk if lumps look imminent. Once the sauce is boiling simmer for 2 minutes, then draw off the heat. Stir in the grated cheese, allowing it to melt.

Sprinkle the aubergine slices with salt and leave them on a plate to disgorge their juices. Rinse them well and pat dry. Roll the meat into a neat sausage shape and wrap it with the larding fat or the rashers of bacon. Then tie it at 3.5-cm/1½-inch intervals with small pieces of string. Slice between the pieces of string so that you get 4 even-sized round veal steaks, each tied with string and surrounded with the bacon or fat.

Set the oven to cool (150°C, 300°F, Gas Mark 2). Dip the aubergines into the seasoned flour and shake off any excess. Melt

177

half the butter and 1 tablespoon of oil in a frying pan and fry the aubergines on both sides until golden brown and tender. Don't fry too fast or the aubergines will brown before the middle is cooked. Take them out and keep warm in the oven. Then dust the veal pieces in the seasoned flour and heat a little more butter and remaining oil in the pan. Fry them for 6–8 minutes on each side or until they are lightly browned and just cooked. Remove the strings and keep the veal warm.

Now put the chopped shallot or onion into the pan and add the rest of the butter. Cook slowly for 2 minutes, then add the paprika and cook again for another 2 minutes. Pour on the wine, mix well and boil rapidly for a minute or so or until the liquid is reduced by about half. Add the cream and salt and pepper to taste and keep warm.

To dish the veal put the aubergine slices in the bottom of a flameproof dish and put a veal steak on top of each one. Spoon the Mornay sauce over the veal and put it under the grill to brown. Heat the wine and paprika sauce and pour it round, not over, the meat.

SERVES FOUR

BLANQUETTE OF VEAL

METRIC/IMPERIAL
1 kg/2 lb pie veal
½ lemon
2 bay leaves
a few parsley stalks
sprig of thyme
stick of celery
pinch of nutmeg
salt and pepper
2 medium onions, sliced
2 carrots, peeled and cut into 5-cm/2-inch sticks
1 teaspoon cornflour
3 egg yolks
150 ml/¼ pint double cream
fried bread triangles
chopped parsley

Cut the veal into small cubes and trim off any skin or gristle. Put it into a pan of water with the piece of lemon, the herbs and celery, tied together with string, a pinch of nutmeg, a little salt and the sliced onion. Bring very slowly to the boil, skimming off any froth or scum that rises to the surface. When the liquid has reached boiling point remove the piece of lemon and turn the heat down so that the liquid barely moves. Cover with a lid and simmer gently for 45 minutes.

Add the carrots and continue cooking for a further 15 minutes–20 minutes. By then the veal should be very tender and the carrots just cooked. Strain the liquid into a jug, throw away the bunch of herbs and put the solid ingredients into an ovenproof serving dish or casserole. Cover with a lid or foil and keep warm.

Mix the cornflour with 1–2 tablespoons of water and pour on a little of the hot stock from the jug. Return the contents of the jug, and the slaked cornflour, to the saucepan and stir steadily until boiling. You should now have a slightly thickened sauce, about the consistency of thin cream. If it is still very watery in consistency do not be tempted to add more cornflour, but simply boil the sauce rapidly until it is reduced to the required consistency.

In a bowl large enough to take the sauce mix the egg yolks and cream together until well blended. Add a tablespoon or so of the hot sauce and mix well. Draw the sauce off the heat and allow it to cool for a few seconds. Then pour it into the bowl while stirring steadily. The egg yolk should cook sufficiently in the hot liquid to thicken the sauce to the consistency of double cream. If it does not, it should be returned to heat, in the saucepan, and stirred constantly until thickened. On no account should it be allowed to come near boiling point, or the eggs will scramble.

Taste the sauce and add salt and pepper as necessary (sea salt and freshly ground white pepper are best). Pour the sauce over the meat and vegetables and surround with the fried bread triangles. Scatter with a little chopped parsley and serve at once.

If the blanquette is to be kept warm in the oven, make sure the temperature is very low, lest the yolks scramble in the sauce.

SERVES FOUR TO FIVE

And simply extravagant. . .

BONED CHICKEN STUFFED WITH LEEKS

This recipe is a fiddle to do, but very low-caloried, so excellent for entertaining weight-conscious guests. It looks amazingly pretty, especially if served cold, cut across into slices.

METRIC/IMPERIAL
1 (1.75-kg/4-lb) roasting chicken
salt and pepper
1 teaspoon chopped tarragon
4 leeks
FOR THE STOCK
bones and giblets of the bird
½ onion, sliced
1 bay leaf
1 stick celery, chopped
1 small carrot, sliced
salt and pepper
FOR THE SAUCE (IF SERVING HOT)
15 g/½ oz butter
15 g/½ oz flour
2–3 tablespoons double cream (optional)
1 tablespoon finely shredded pale green leek to garnish
FOR THE ASPIC (IF SERVING COLD)
7 g/¼ oz powdered gelatine
2 egg whites, and the egg shells
6 or 7 fresh tarragon leaves *or* thin strips of cucumber skin to garnish

Split the skin of the bird from the neck to the pope's nose along the backbone. Using a short sharp knife work your way round the bird releasing the skin and the flesh from the carcase. Do not worry if you cut into the flesh by mistake: the odd bits of flesh can be used in the stuffing. When you get to the wings and legs work the bones out from both ends, cutting off the pinions and the knobbly ends of the drumsticks. Take care throughout the boning operation not to pierce the skin with the point of the knife. When you have finished you will have a rather unsightly floppy piece of skin and chicken. Lay it skin side down on a board.

Scrape any remaining flesh from the bones and put it on top of the chicken. Put the bones in a very large saucepan with all the other stock ingredients, and cover with water. Boil rapidly while you deal with the chicken.

Sprinkle the inside of the chicken with salt, pepper, and the tarragon. Wash the leeks, cutting off most of the green part. Wash the green leaves too and add them to the stock. You should be left with 4 leeks, white part only, about 10–13 cm/4–5 inches long. Lay these down the middle of the chicken and fold the sides over like a parcel. If the edges of the chicken skin barely meet sew up along the edge, but if they overlap slightly don't bother. Wrap the chicken fairly tightly in a piece of muslin and tie the ends. Now put the chicken parcel on top of the bones in the stock saucepan, turn the heat down to simmer and put on a well-fitting lid. Simmer very gently for about 1 hour or until a skewer will pass with little resistance through chicken and leeks.

To serve hot: carefully unwrap the chicken and put it on a warmed serving dish. Serve with some of the skimmed stock as a sauce, or if a richer sauce is required thicken 300 ml/½ pint of the stock (which must have all the fat removed from it) with the butter and flour kneaded together: to do this drop the butter-flour paste into the boiling stock bit by bit, whisking vigorously as you do so. Adjust the seasoning and add the cream if liked. Drop the shredded leek into boiling water for half a minute, or until it is bright green and slightly softened. Scatter the leek shreds over the chicken and spoon over either a ladleful of hot skimmed stock, or, if used, the creamy sauce. Serve immediately.

If serving the chicken cold: you can serve it simply sliced across into rounds, arranged prettily on a plate. Or you can give it a shiny aspic coating, which looks very professional but is rather more effort to do.

TO MAKE THE ASPIC Strain the stock when you take the chicken from it and allow to cool. Put it in a bowl in the refrigerator overnight, or while the chicken is cooling, so that the fat on the top will solidify and make it easy to remove. If the stock has set to a firm jelly you need not add the gelatine, but if it is at all runny you must do so.

Put the fat-free stock into a very large saucepan and warm gently until liquid, but not hot. Sprinkle the gelatine over the surface of the liquid, and allow to stand, off the heat, for 10 minutes. Then bring the stock to the boil. If the gelatine is not used the stock can be heated straight away. When the stock is hot, but not yet boiling, whisk the egg whites until frothy and crush the eggshells finely. Add eggshells and whites to the stock pan and, using a balloon whisk, whisk steadily while the stock comes to the boil.

When the egg white on top of the liquid begins to set into a solid mass and the stock and egg white 'head' rises in the pan, remove the whisk and allow the stock to rise as high as you dare. Then gently draw the pan off the heat and allow it to subside. On no account must you stir the stock at this stage for fear of breaking the egg white head, which is to act as a filter in clearing the stock. Put the pan back on the heat and again let the stock bubble up and the head rise. Do this three times in all and then leave the stock to settle for 10 minutes or so.

Stretch a double piece of muslin over a large clean bucket or bowl and secure it with a tough rubber band, or with string. Alternatively, line a wide cook's sieve with muslin or two J-cloths and fix it over a bowl. Now tilt the saucepan, allowing the egg white head to slip into the sieve or on to the muslin. Then pour the stock, very slowly, through egg white and muslin which between them should filter the stock absolutely crystal clear. If it emerges murky, repeat the process. Don't hurry it by squeezing or stirring the contents of the muslin – this will certainly give you murky jelly. When all the stock is through cool it until on the point of setting.

Put the chicken on a wire rack over a tray. Paint the surface of it (using an absolutely clean brush) with the cooled aspic. Arrange the tarragon leaves, or fine shreds of cucumber skin, on the back of the chicken as a neat decoration. Put the chicken in the refrigerator until the decoration is set firmly in place. Then carefully give it another coating of just-liquid aspic. This will give a shine to the surface. Successive paintings with aspic will build up a thickish layer, but they're not necessary, and in my opinion too heavy a coating of aspic is unattractive.

Set the rest of the aspic in a shallow tray. When well set, cut it with a knife into even-sized small squares. Put the chicken on a serving plate and using a fish slice surround with the diced aspic. Keep refrigerated until needed.

SERVES SIX TO EIGHT

BALLOTINE OF CHICKEN

METRIC/IMPERIAL
1 (1.75-kg/4-lb) roasting chicken
15 g/½ oz butter
FOR THE FILLING
175 g/6 oz minced veal
175 g/6 oz minced belly of pork
1 onion, finely chopped
75 g/3 oz chicken livers
1 clove garlic, chopped
1 teaspoon rubbed dried sage *or* 2 teaspoons fresh sage
1 tablespoon pistachio nuts
25 g/1 oz butter
100 g/4 oz cooked ham, finely diced
salt and freshly ground black pepper

Follow the procedure for boning the chicken described in the previous recipe and fill it with the following stuffing:

Melt the butter in a frying pan and in it soften the chopped onion and garlic. Add the chicken livers with all discoloured parts removed and turn up the heat to fry fairly fast until lightly browned. Mash the livers with a fork. Now mix all the stuffing ingredients together and use to stuff the chicken. Draw the sides of the chicken up and sew together with thread or fine string. Put the bird, sewn-side down, into a roasting tin and spread it lightly with butter. Season with freshly ground black pepper. Roast in a moderate over (180°C, 350°F, Gas Mark 4) for 1½–1¾ hours, or until the chicken is golden brown and a skewer will glide easily into the stuffing. Remove the thread. Serve hot with gravy, or well chilled and cut in slices.

SERVES FOUR TO SIX

And simply extravagant. . .

WHOLE BONED TURKEY STUFFED WITH BOILED GAMMON

If the turkey is to be stuffed the day before cooking, ingredients must be as chilled as possible, and the turkey must be kept refrigerated. The stuffed cooked turkey is excellent cold. Serve it with pickled fruit or chutney.

METRIC/IMPERIAL
1 (2.75-kg/6-lb) piece of boneless smoked gammon
2 carrots
1 onion
2 bay leaves
parsley stalks
8 peppercorns
1 (6.75-kg/15-lb) turkey
FOR THE STUFFING
25 g/1 oz butter
1 large onion, finely chopped
900 g/2 lb sausage meat
900 g/2 lb unsweetened chestnut purée (canned is fine)
225 g/8 oz fresh white breadcrumbs
1 teaspoon dried sage
2 tablespoons chopped parsley
salt and freshly ground black pepper
1 egg, lightly beaten
FOR ROASTING
50 g/2 oz butter
1 onion, sliced
2 bay leaves
2 parsley stalks
600 ml/1 pint water
FOR THE GRAVY
about 2 tablespoons flour
300 ml/½ pint turkey stock *or* vegetable water
FOR THE GARNISH
bunch of watercress

Soak the gammon in cold water overnight to remove the excess salt. Place it in a large pan of cold water and add the carrots, onion, bay leaves, parsley stalks and peppercorns, and slowly bring up to the boil. Cover and simmer for 25 minutes per half kilo/per lb. Leave to cool slightly in the stock, then lift out and pull off the skin. Leave to get completely cold.

First bone the turkey. You will need a very sharp small knife. Chop off the legs just above the knee joint. Using the little knife, work the skin and flesh loose from the bone, pressing the flesh back all the time to expose the bone. It is a combination of loosening the flesh by inserting the knife, and scraping the bone with the blade of the knife to press back the flesh. When you have gone as far as you can with both legs do the same to the wing joints, starting above the pinion joint. Then work on both ends of the turkey, always trying to keep the knife as close to the carcase as possible so as not to pierce the skin.

You will find that you can work the carcase loose with your fingers, easing between the skin and bone. When the whole carcase is loose detach it from the legs and wings and draw it out through the large opening – not through the neck. Now turn the whole turkey inside out and detach the leg and wing bones. Turn right side out again and stuff it, making sure that any meat still attached to the bones is added to the stuffing.

To make the stuffing: melt the butter, add the onion and cook until soft, but not coloured. Using your hands mix together the sausage meat, chestnut purée, breadcrumbs, sage, parsley and salt and pepper to taste. Add enough egg to bind the mixture together, but do not get it sloppy.

Push the ham (cut in two if necessary) into the turkey through the large cavity at the vent end of the bird. Using your hands push all the stuffing into the turkey and around the ham. What you are trying to do is restore the turkey to its original shape, so pack plenty of stuffing into the breast and any gaps around the ham. Sew up both ends of the turkey with needle and thin string.

Smear the butter all over the bird and put it into the roasting tin. Add all the giblets except the liver. Add the onion, bay leaves and parsley stalks. Pour in the water.

Roast the bird in a moderately hot oven (200°C, 400°F, Gas Mark 6) for 1 hour, then lower the temperature to 180°C, 350°F, Gas Mark 4, and roast for a further 3 hours. Baste occasionally as it cooks, and cover with foil or greaseproof paper if it is browning too much. When the turkey is cooked, that is when the juices from the thigh part run clear if pierced with a skewer, transfer to a serving dish and keep warm.

Skim the fat from the pan juices. Whisk in a tablespoon or so of flour and bring, stirring, to the boil. Strain into a warmed gravy boat.

Garnish the turkey with the watercress.

SERVES FIFTEEN

And simply extravagant. . .

MARMALADE DUCK

*This is a little like famous Bigarade duck, made with Bigarade bitter
oranges. If you cannot get bitter oranges like Seville, add 1 tablespoon
lemon juice.*

METRIC/IMPERIAL
1 (2.25-kg/5-lb) duckling
1 tablespoon soy sauce
2 tablespoons marmalade
1 shallot, very finely chopped
1 teaspoon butter
2 tablespoons orange juice (preferably from a Seville orange)
200 ml/7 fl oz stock made from the neck and giblets (except the liver)
1 teaspoon cornflour
salt and pepper

Prick the duck all over with a sharp skewer or fork. Rub it inside and
out and with salt, and roast it, without fat, for 1 hour in a hot oven
(220°C, 425°F, Gas Mark 7), turning over once during cooking, and
pouring away the fat.

Take out the duck, pour off the fat from the tin, but not any duck
juices. Tip the juices from inside the duck into the tin, and put back
the duck, breast side up. Paint it all over with half the soy sauce and
marmalade. Return to the oven and cook, without basting, until the
skin is a good brown and the duck is tender and cooked, 15–30
minutes.

While the duck is cooking, fry the shallot in the butter, until just
pale brown. Add the duck liver, chopped, and fry fast for two
minutes. Add the orange juice, the rest of the soy sauce and the
marmalade, and set aside. Mix a little of the cold stock (or 1
tablespoon water) with the cornflour, pour on the rest of the stock,
mix well and add to the pan with the liver, etc. Stir well, while
bringing to the boil. Simmer until a thin syrupy consistency is
reached. Add salt and pepper to taste.

When the duck is cooked, lift it on to a serving dish, first tipping
any juices from the cavity into the sauce. Pour off the fat from the
roasting tin, and skim any remaining fat carefully, then add the duck
juices from the tin to the sauce. Reheat and serve with the crisp
duck, handed round separately.

SERVES THREE TO FOUR

STUFFED BONED DUCK WITH GREEN OLIVES

METRIC/IMPERIAL

1 (2.25–2.75-kg/5–6-lb) fresh duck
about 25 g/1 oz butter
1 onion, finely chopped
225 g/8 oz belly of pork, minced
4 large slices white bread, made into breadcrumbs
1 whole egg and 1 egg yolk
1 teaspoon chopped or rubbed sage
1 clove garlic, crushed
2 tablespoons green olives, stoned and chopped
salt and pepper
1 orange

Bone the duck: cut through the skin all the way down the backbone. Work the flesh away from the carcase doing first one side and then the other. When you come to the legs, cut off the knobbly drumstick joint and work the bones out. Chop the pinions off the wings and work the wing bones out too. You should end up with a large uneven square of skin, with flesh attached. Put this, skin side down, on a board. If there is any flesh still adhering to the carcase or limb joints, scrape this off and put it back in the duck.

To make the stuffing: melt the butter in a frying pan and add the chopped onion. Cook until soft and transparent. Trim the discoloured part from the duck liver (it would make the stuffing bitter). Cut the liver into shreds and add it to the onions. Cook for 2 minutes over a moderate heat.

Put the minced pork and the breadcrumbs into a large bowl and add the contents of the frying pan, the whole egg and yolk, the sage, garlic, olives and plenty of salt and pepper. Finely grate the rind of the orange and add that too. Squeeze the juice and add enough of it to produce a stuffing of a dropping consistency. Put the stuffing on to the bird, down the middle. Bring the sides of the duck up and sew them together so that you have a long parcel.

Put the duck in a lightly greased bread tin, or a narrow pan, or a roasting tin with a bread tin next to it so that the duck is supported and held into a not-too-flattened shape. Roast in a moderately hot oven (200°C, 400°F, Gas Mark 6) for 1–1½ hours, pouring away the fat that accumulates occasionally, until the bird is brown and crisp all over and a skewer penetrates the thigh part with ease. Serve hot or cold.   SERVES SIX

And simply extravagant. . .

GALANTINE OF PHEASANT

METRIC/IMPERIAL
1 large pheasant, preferably a hen
225 g/8 oz raw chicken meat, minced
100 g/4 oz belly of pork, minced
50 g/2 oz fresh white breadcrumbs
1 onion, finely chopped
2 tablespoons Marsala
1 tablespoon chopped parsley
salt and freshly ground black pepper
1 slice cooked ham, cut into strips
1 slice cooked tongue, cut into strips
1 large mushroom, sliced
FOR THE COOKING STOCK
few slices of carrot
few slices onion
few slices celery
1 teaspoon peppercorns
1 bay leaf
small bunch of parsley
salt
pinch of thyme
900 ml/1½ pints water
FOR THE ASPIC
15 g/½ oz powdered gelatine
1 or 2 egg whites, and the egg shells
FOR THE DECORATION
2 button mushrooms, sliced
strip of cucumber skin
2 or 3 stuffed olives, sliced

To bone the pheasant: first cut off its head, then cut through the skin from the parson's nose to the head all along the backbone. With a short sharp knife work the skin and flesh away from the carcase keeping as close to the bones as possible and working back the flesh as you go. Do first one side and then the other. Chop the drumstick knuckle end off, and the wing pinions. Work the leg and wing bones out. At the end you should have a flat square of pheasant's skin and flesh, hopefully with the skin unpierced anywhere. Put the bones in a pan and add all the stock ingredients. Bring to the boil and simmer for 30 minutes.

In a large bowl mix together the raw chicken meat, the minced belly of pork, breadcrumbs, chopped onion, Marsala and chopped parsley and add plenty of salt and freshly ground black pepper. Open the pheasant up and lay it on a board with the skin side down. Spread half the stuffing over it and lay on it the strips of ham, tongue, and the sliced mushroom. Cover with the rest of the stuffing. Sew up the bird with needle and thread, then wrap the pheasant parcel in a clean piece of muslin and tie the ends together.

Strain the stock into a heavy-bottomed saucepan and put the pheasant into it. Cover tightly with a well-fitting lid and simmer for 1½ hours or until the pheasant is tender. Lift out the bird and strain the stock into a bowl. Re-wrap the bird in the muslin, this time more tightly, squeezing until some of the juices from inside the bird begin to run out. Alternatively wrap another muslin cloth, or a tea towel, round the bird on top of the first muslin and squeeze well. Allow it to cool, and then refrigerate well. Refrigerate the stock overnight too so that the fat can set, making it easier to remove the next day.

If the stock, when cold, sets into a good jelly there is no need to use gelatine but if it is at all runny put it into a clean saucepan and sprinkle over the gelatine.

To make the aspic: follow the method for Boned Chicken Stuffed with Leeks (see page 180), using 600 ml/1 pint stock.

When the aspic is on the point of setting unwrap the cold pheasant and place it on a wire rack with a plate or tray underneath it. Using a clean brush or a spoon carefully coat the pheasant all over with a layer of aspic. Decorate the pheasant with slices of button mushroom, small leaves made out of peelings of cucumber and thin slices of the stuffed olives. Put back into the refrigerator to set the decoration. Then coat with a further layer of aspic. Allow that to set solidly, and add one more layer if necessary.

Set the remaining aspic in a shallow tray and then chop it or cut into small dice. Dish the pheasant on a serving plate and surround with the chopped aspic. Keep cool until needed.

SERVES SIX

PARTRIDGE AND CABBAGE PIE

METRIC/IMPERIAL
3 partridges
butter for frying
4 tablespoons each of brandy and Madeira
1 large Savoy cabbage
4 rashers streaky bacon, with rind removed
225 g/8 oz belly of pork, minced
salt and freshly ground black pepper
pinch of sage
garlic (optional)
juniper berries (optional)
100 g/4 oz smoked pork
FOR THE STOCK
1 bay leaf
1–2 slices onion
1 carrot
bunch of parsley
FOR THE SAUCE
1 tablespoon tomato purée
25 g/1 oz chicken liver pâté

Fry the partridges fairly quickly in butter for 5 minutes on each side, so that they are well browned. Pour in the brandy and the Madeira and set alight. Leave the birds in the pan to cool so that you can collect any juices that run from them.

Briefly cook the washed cabbage leaves in boiling water for 2–3 minutes, then lift them out, keeping the water. Butter a large china or ovenproof pie dish or casserole and lay the rashers of bacon in it. Line the dish with 10 or 12 of the cabbage leaves.

Cut the flesh from the partridges and put the breast meat into the dish inside the cabbage lining. Pour on any pan juices. Mince the leg meat and mix it with the minced pork. Flavour with salt, pepper and a little sage (and crushed garlic or juniper if you like). With floured hands roll this mixture into tiny sausages. Fry these quickly, to brown them only, in butter or bacon fat and add to the partridge meat.

Dice the smoked pork and fry it briefly in the pan too, then add a little of the cabbage water, cover the pan and allow to simmer for 10 minutes. Lift out the smoked pork pieces and add them to the other meats. Put the partridge bones, with the bay leaf, onion, carrot and the bunch of parsley, into a saucepan and cover with water (preferably that in which you cooked the cabbage). Simmer for 45 minutes.

Spoon the stock from simmering the smoked pork over the meat in the pie. Sprinkle in some pepper and cover with a layer of cabbage leaves. Stand the dish in a roasting tin of hot water and cover with buttered foil. Bake in a moderate oven (180°C, 350°F, Gas Mark 4) for 1½ hours.

Meanwhile make the sauce: reduce the partridge stock to 150 ml/¼ pint by rapid boiling. Strain it into a clean saucepan, season to taste, and slowly beat in the tomato purée and pâté.

Turn the pie out, upside down, on a serving dish and pour over the hot sauce.

SERVES SIX TO EIGHT

QUAILS WITH RAISINS, WALNUTS AND GRAPES

METRIC/IMPERIAL
8 plump quails, cleaned
4 rashers streaky bacon, with rind removed
175 ml/6 fl oz stock
1 onion, chopped
1 bay leaf
few sprigs of parsley
3 tablespoons white wine
salt and pepper
1 heaped teaspoon flour
100 g/4 oz seedless grapes *or* green grapes, halved and seeded
25 g/1 oz walnuts, roughly chopped
1 tablespoon raisins
2 tablespoons double cream
few sprigs of watercress for garnish

Cut each bacon rasher in half and put a piece over each quail breast. Put the quail in a roasting tin and pour in the stock. Add the onion, bay leaf, parsley sprigs and white wine. Season with salt and pepper. Roast the quail in a moderately hot oven (200°C, 400°F, Gas Mark 6) for 15 minutes, then remove the bacon and continue cooking for a further 10 minutes, when the quails should be pale brown and very tender. Put the quails on a serving dish, cover and keep warm while you make the gravy.

Heat the juices from the tin and strain them. Skim off any fat into a teacup. Mix this fat to a paste with the teaspoon of flour. Pour some of the hot stock into the cup, mixing well. Then return the flour mixture and the hot stock to a saucepan or the roasting tin and stir steadily until boiling. Check the seasoning and add salt and pepper if necessary. Then add the grapes, the walnuts and the raisins. Reheat and stir in the cream.

Spoon the sauce over the quails and garnish with the watercress.

SERVES FOUR OR EIGHT

ROAST GROUSE

A single grouse is sometimes served for 2 people, but I think it is the most delicious of all game birds, and am very resentful if I have to share it!

METRIC/IMPERIAL
4 grouse (preferably hen birds)
butter
4 or 5 rashers streaky bacon
100 ml/4 fl oz sweet red wine (such as Spanish Tarragona)
salt and freshly ground black pepper
FOR THE BREADCRUMBS
50 g/2 oz fresh white breadcrumbs
50 g/2 oz butter
TO SERVE
bread sauce
game chips *or* game chip baskets
watercress to garnish

Put the birds in a big roasting tin and spread them with butter. Then cover the breasts with the streaky bacon and pour in the wine. Roast the birds in a moderately hot oven (200°C, 400°F, Gas Mark 6), basting frequently, for 35 minutes or until they are still slightly pink inside (pick one up, turn it over and make a small cut under the leg to investigate). Ten minutes before the grouse are due to come out remove the bacon pieces to allow the breasts to brown. When they are done (if you prefer them cooked through, increase the cooking time by 10 or 15 minutes), take them out and keep them warm on a serving dish.

Boil up the juices in the tin, add salt and pepper and pour into a gravy boat, or around the birds.

To make the breadcrumbs, simply fry them in the butter until brown. They need frequent turning and stirring or the bottom ones will brown while the top ones are still wet and soft. When they are all brown and crisp put them into a warmed small bowl.

Dish the grouse garnished with the watercress, and pass the game chips, the bread sauce and breadcrumbs separately.

SERVES FOUR OR EIGHT

GAME CHIPS

I must confess that I never make game chips any more. I simply buy a large packet of potato crisps, sprinkle them with salt and heat them up in the oven. But take care that you don't end up with one of the nastier varieties like 'bacon flavour' or 'cheese 'n onion'. If you want to make you own, here goes.

METRIC/IMPERIAL
450 g/1 lb large potatoes
fat for deep-frying
salt

Peel the potatoes and slice them in wafer-thin slices. As you slice them sink them in cold water until you are ready to fry them.

Heat the oil until a crumb will sizzle vigorously in it. Just before frying dry the potato slices thoroughly on a tea towel. Fry a few handfuls at a time until crisp and pale brown. Drain them well on absorbent paper and sprinkle with salt.

SERVES FOUR

BREAD SAUCE

METRIC/IMPERIAL
50–75 g/2–3 oz breadcrumbs
300 ml/½ pint milk
½ onion, stuck with 3 cloves
salt and pepper
25 g/1 oz butter

Heat the milk and pour on to the crumbs. Sink the onion with its cloves in the mixture and leave for 1 hour or so. When you are ready to serve the sauce reheat it, remove the onion and add more milk if necessary. It should not be stodgy but should be the consistency of sloppy porridge. Add salt and pepper to taste, and lastly stir in the butter.

MAKES 300 ML/½ PINT

GAME CHIP BASKETS

METRIC/IMPERIAL
450 g/1 lb large potatoes
oil for deep-frying
40 g/1½ oz butter
1 (574-g/1 lb 5-oz) can whole unsweetened chestnuts
handful of raisins
small bunch of white seedless grapes (or grapes with seeds removed)
½ tablespoon pine nuts

Slice the potatoes as for game chips. If you have a mandolin slicer or some slicer that will give you frilly flat game chips, use it. Dip a wire sieve, a little larger than a small ladle, into the fat to get it well greased and then line it with overlapping raw game chips. Now put a metal ladle (also dipped in the fat) into the strainer to hold the chips in place. Fry them holding them in this position. When the 'basket' is crisp and golden take it out and drain it on absorbent paper. Then make the next one and so on.

Melt the butter in a frying pan and add the well-drained chestnuts, the raisins, grapes and pine nuts. Shake over the heat until hot and just beginning to brown.

Just before serving fill the game chip baskets with this mixture and serve at once.

SERVES FOUR

Puddings

ATHOLL BROSE

Classically, Atholl Brose was made of oatmeal and was served hot. But this is a good, chilled, modern version – a light but rich after-dinner pud.

METRIC/IMPERIAL
300 ml/½ pint double cream
4 tablespoons whisky
3 tablespoons runny honey

Whip the cream until stiff and then stir in the honey and the whisky. Spoon into individual small glasses or cups and chill well before serving.   SERVES FOUR

CHOCOLATE MOUSSE WITH ORANGE

METRIC/IMPERIAL
3 eggs
25 g/1 oz castor sugar
175 g/6 oz dark sweetened chocolate
2 tablespoons orange juice
finely grated rind of 1 orange
15 g/½ oz butter, melted

Separate the eggs and beat the yolks with the sugar until light and fluffy. Put the chocolate and orange juice into a heavy-bottomed saucepan and heat slowly, stirring, until you have a smooth mixture of the consistency of double cream. Cool it slightly and then beat into the yolk mixture. Add the grated orange rind and the melted butter.

Whisk the egg whites until they are stiff but not dry. Fold them into the chocolate mixture and spoon into a dish to set. Leave at least 5 hours before serving.   SERVES FOUR

And simply extravagant. . .

GREEN FRUIT SALAD

*This fruit salad is particularly good served with a ginger syllabub mixture
instead of whipped cream (see page 139). If it is served on its own, a dash
of Kirsch in the syrup is good.*

METRIC/IMPERIAL
1 kg/2 lb any green fruit, e.g. melon, cut into chunks or scooped into
balls
green grapes, halved and seeded
greengages, split and stoned
green apples, sliced with the skin left on
Kiwi fruit (Chinese gooseberries), sliced
FOR THE SYRUP
450 ml/¾ pint water
175 g/6 oz granulated sugar
2 tablespoons lemon juice

Make the syrup first. Put the sugar and water together in a saucepan
and bring slowly to the boil. Once the sugar has melted, boil the
syrup rapidly until it feels slightly tacky when tested between finger
and thumb. Add the lemon juice and allow it to cool. Prepare the
fruit, dropping it straight into the syrup to prevent discoloration.
Chill well before serving.

SERVES FOUR TO SIX

BRANDY SNAP CUPS

This recipe is made from the same mixture as the more usual brandy snaps, but instead of being rolled round a stick to form a cigarette shape, they are moulded to form small cups which are then filled.

METRIC/IMPERIAL
100 g/4 oz sugar
100 g/4 oz butter
4 tablespoons golden syrup
100 g/4 oz flour
juice of ½ lemon
large pinch of ground ginger
TO FILL
ice cream or whipped cream

Set the oven to moderate (180°C, 350°F, Gas Mark 4). Grease a baking tray, the blade of a palette knife and one end of a wide rolling pin or a narrow jam jar or bottle.

Melt the sugar, butter and syrup together, then remove from the heat. Sift in the flour, stirring well as you do so. Now add the lemon juice and the ginger and put the mixture out on the baking tray in small teaspoonfuls at least 15 cm/6 inches apart. Bake for 5–7 minutes when they will be golden brown but still very soft. Watch carefully because the edges burn easily.

Remove the baking tray from the oven and as soon as cool enough to handle lever each biscuit off the baking tray with the palette knife and shape it round the end of the rolling pin or greased jam jar to form a cup-shaped mould. As soon as it has set in the right shape ease it off the end of the pin or mould and leave on a wire rack to get quite cold. Serve filled with ice cream or with whipped cream.

NOTE If brandy snaps are not to be served immediately, they must be stored in a totally airtight container. Make sure they are stone cold before putting them away.

SERVES FOUR TO SIX

PEACH SHORTCAKE

METRIC/IMPERIAL
75 g/3 oz hazelnuts
100 g/4oz butter
75 g/3 oz castor sugar
150 ml/5 oz flour
good pinch of salt
300 ml/½ pint whipped cream
4 fresh peaches
icing sugar

Put the hazelnuts into a hot oven. When they are browned put them into a clean tea towel and rub well to remove the skins. Grind the nuts in an electric blender or nut-grinder, taking care not to overdo it – you do not want to mash them or extract the oils.

Put the butter and sugar together in a bowl and beat until light, pale in colour and fluffy. Sift the flour and the salt into the mixture and add the nuts. Fold together carefully. Chill for 30 minutes or so until firm enough to handle.

Divide the pastry into three and press with your hands, or with a rolling pin, into three flat rounds the size of a dessert plate. Slide them on to baking trays and bake in a moderately hot oven (190°C, 375°F, Gas Mark 5) for 12 minutes, or until a little brown at the edges and biscuit-coloured in the middle. Cool slightly before removing them to a wire rack. While one of them is still warm cut it into 6 or 8 segments.

Whip the cream until stiff. Skin and slice the peaches into the cream, folding them together. Using half this mixture as a filling, sandwich the two whole rounds of pastry together and put on a serving plate. Spread the other half of the filling on top and stick the cut segments of pastry into the cream, each one at a slight angle. Dust with icing sugar just before serving.

SERVES FOUR TO SIX

APRICOT CHEESECAKE

METRIC/IMPERIAL
FOR THE CRUST
175 g/6 oz digestive biscuits
75 g/3 oz butter, melted
good pinch of cinnamon
25 g/1 oz castor sugar
FOR THE FILLING
2 tablespoons water
15 g/½ oz powdered gelatine
1 (425-g/15-oz) can apricots
225 g/8 oz soft full-fat cream cheese
150 ml/¼ pint double cream, whipped
3 tablespoons soured cream
about 40–50 g/1½–2 oz castor sugar
finely grated rind and juice of ½ lemon
FOR THE DECORATION
150 ml/¼ pint double cream, whipped
few apricot halves
1 tablespoon chopped almonds, browned

Mix the ingredients for the crust together and press it into the bottom of a 20-cm/8-inch flan dish. Press down firmly and refrigerate for 20 minutes.

Put the water into a small heavy saucepan and sprinkle on the gelatine. Leave to soak for 10 minutes.

Drain the apricots and reserve 3 or 4 for decoration. Put the rest into an electric blender and whizz until smooth. Alternatively, push them through a sieve. Mix them with the remaining filling ingredients. Leave at room temperature.

When the gelatine looks spongy put it over gentle heat and warm until it is runny and clear. Stir it into the filling mixture. Spoon the mixture into the flan dish on top of the biscuit base and refrigerate until set. Decorate the top with the whipped cream, reserved apricot halves and the chopped nuts.

SERVES FOUR TO SIX

And simply extravagant. . .

CHOCOLATE AND ORANGE CAKE

METRIC/IMPERIAL
300 ml/½ pint milk
350 g/12 oz soft brown sugar
1 teaspoon vanilla essence
75 g/3 oz dark sweetened chocolate
finely grated rind of ½ orange
100 g/4 oz butter
2 eggs
225 g/8 oz plain flour
1 teaspoon bicarbonate of soda
FOR THE FILLING
300 ml/½ pint double cream
grated rind of ½ orange
castor sugar
FOR THE ICING
100 g/4 oz dark chocolate
about 4 tablespoons milk

Line the bottom of three 20–23-cm/8–9-inch sandwich tins with greaseproof paper and brush them lightly with melted butter. Put half the milk into a saucepan and add half the sugar, the vanilla essence, the chocolate (broken up) and the grated orange rind. Stir over gentle heat until the mixture is smooth.

In a large bowl beat the butter with the remaining sugar until very light, pale and moussey. Beat in the eggs one at a time and then add the milky chocolate mixture and beat again. Sift in the flour with the bicarbonate of soda and mix well. Then add the rest of the milk and stir.

Divide the mixture evenly between the cake tins. Bake in a moderately hot oven (190°C, 375°F, Gas Mark 5) for about 30 minutes or until the cake looks slightly shrivelled round the edges. Don't worry if it still feels very soft – it is meant to be a very moist cake. Cool in the tin for about 5 minutes before turning out on a wire rack. Then peel off the paper stuck to the back.

Whip the cream and add the orange rind and enough sugar to sweeten to your satisfaction. When the cake is stone cold use this flavoured cream to sandwich the three layers together.

To make the icing: put the chocolate into a saucepan and add the milk. Heat slowly, stirring all the time until smooth and thick. Pour it over the cake, spreading with a palette knife if necessary.

SERVES SIX

GÂTEAU ST. HONORÉ

A monster version of this cake is generally served as a French wedding cake. This quantity, however, is more moderate.

METRIC/IMPERIAL
FOR THE PASTRY
150 g/6 oz flour
pinch of salt
75 g/3 oz butter
3 egg yolks
75 g/3 oz sugar
vanilla essence
FOR THE PROFITEROLES
75 g/3 oz butter
225 ml/7½ fl oz water
3 small eggs, lightly beaten
95 g/3¾ oz flour
FOR THE CUSTARD FILLING
2 egg yolks
50 g/2 oz castor sugar
20 g/¾ oz flour
20 g/¾ oz cornflour
2 drops vanilla essence
300 ml/½ pint milk
FOR THE CARAMEL
100 g/4 oz granulated sugar

Start with the pastry. Allow the butter to soften out of the refrigerator. Sift the flour into a large bowl and make a well in the centre. Put the salt and softened butter into the middle and put the egg yolks on top of the butter. Pour the sugar in the middle as well and add a few drops of vanilla essence.

Now using the fingertips of one hand only, pinch and mix the sugar, yolks, etc. in the middle until they are a smooth sticky paste. Gradually incorporate the surrounding flour into a mixture and knead lightly until the pastry is smooth. Chill while you make the profiteroles.

Set the oven to moderately hot (200°C, 400°F, Gas Mark 6). Put the butter and the water together in a medium-sized saucepan, and heat slowly. Once the butter has melted bring the mixture to a rapid boil. As soon as it is boiling tip in all the flour at once and draw the pan off the heat. Using a wooden spoon beat the mixture vigorously until it is quite smooth, and inclined to leave the sides of the pan. Allow to cool for about 10 minutes.

Now beat the eggs into the mixture, a little at a time. First of all the mixture will go slippery and difficult to handle, then become sticky again and finally rather stiff. Continue adding beaten egg until you have a smooth mixture of dropping consistency – it should fall off the spoon in blobs, rather reluctantly.

Wet a large baking tray and put the mixture on to it in smallish dessertspoon balls, about 13 cm/5 inches apart. Bake in the oven until fairly brown and well risen – about 20 minutes. As soon as the profiteroles come out of the oven make a fairly large hole at the side of the base of each one, large enough to allow the steamy air inside to escape, and to use later to fill with custard.

Use the raw pastry to line an 18-cm/7-inch flan ring. Line it with a double layer of greaseproof paper and fill with rice, beans, pebbles or pennies – anything to keep it from bubbling up during cooking. Bake in a moderately hot oven (200°C, 400°F, Gas Mark 6) until slightly brown round the edges. Then lift out the paper and 'blind' beans and return the pastry case to the oven for about 5–10 minutes to finish cooking and drying out. Allow it to cool on a wire rack.

Now the custard. Put the yolks, sugar, both the flours and the vanilla essence into a fairly large, heavy-bottomed saucepan. Mix them well with a wooden spoon until smooth. Add the milk and stir over gentle heat until thick. The mixture will go alarmingly lumpy at first, but will eventually become smooth. Remove from the heat and cool.

Once both the profiteroles and the custard filling are stone cold you can proceed. If the custard mixture is stodgy and thick, beat a little more milk into it. It should be soft.

Fill the mixture into a piping bag fitted with a plain 5-mm/¼-inch nozzle. Using this, fill about two-thirds of the custard into the profiteroles, filling them through the hole previously made to allow the steam to escape. Spread the rest of the custard into the cold flan case.

Now make the caramel: put the sugar into a heavy, fairly wide saucepan. Allow it to melt slowly and then to caramelise to a pale brown toffee. As soon as this stage is reached, dip the tops of the profiteroles, one by one, into the caramel (wear gloves or use tongs – it is dangerously hot) and put them immediately on top of the custard in the pastry case. As you proceed with the profiteroles build up a small castle with them, using the caramel to stick them together. Pour any remaining caramel in a thin trickle all over the cake. Allow it to cool before serving.

SERVES FOUR TO FIVE

CHOCOLATE ROULADE

This is a famous Cordon Bleu recipe, a flourless cake. It must be made a day in advance.

METRIC/IMPERIAL
5 eggs
150 g/5 oz castor sugar
225 g/8 oz dark sweetened chocolate
1 teaspoon instant coffee
4½ tablespoons water
300 ml/½ pint double cream
icing sugar

Line a Swiss roll tin, 23 by 33 cm/9 by 13 inches, with a double layer of greaseproof paper. Snip the corners so that the greaseproof paper will lie flat in the tin. Brush it out lightly with oil. Separate the eggs, putting the yolks in one bowl with the sugar, and the whites in another. Put the chocolate, with the instant coffee and the water, into a saucepan over very gentle heat.

Beat the yolks and sugar until very light and moussey. Stir the chocolate over the heat until you have an absolutely smooth creamy consistency. Stir this into the yolks and sugar mixture. Whisk the egg whites until stiff but not dry. Fold the whites into the chocolate mixture with a large metal spoon. Take care not to overmix. Pour this mixture into the Swiss roll tin and using the spoon break any over-large pockets of egg white.

Bake in a hot oven (220°C, 425°F, Gas Mark 7) for 12–14 minutes or until the top is slightly browned and firm to the touch (the inside will still be squashy, but don't worry). Take the tin from the oven and leave to cool overnight.

The next day whip the cream until it is stiff enough to hold its shape and spread evenly all over the cake. Roll the cake up like a Swiss roll, peeling the backing paper off as you go. The cake is very moist inside, and inclined to break apart. Don't worry about this, just keep going. The icing sugar will cover a multitude of cracks. Besides it is meant to look like a log, and logs often have cracked bark. Put the roulade on to a serving plate. Just before serving dust it lightly with icing sugar.

SERVES FOUR TO SIX

And simply extravagant. . .

CRÈME BRÛLÉE

In the Cheap Puddings section there is a Cheat's Crème Brûlée (page 72).
This is the real thing.

METRIC/IMPERIAL
FOR THE CUSTARD
300 ml/1 pint double cream
1 vanilla pod *or* 4 or 5 drops vanilla essence
4 egg yolks
50 g/2 oz castor sugar
FOR THE CARAMEL
50 g/2 oz castor sugar

Start the day before. Put the cream and vanilla pod, or vanilla essence, into a saucepan and heat up to scalding point, but do not boil. Beat the yolks and sugar until smooth. Pour the hot cream on to the yolks, stirring as you do so.

Put the mixture into the top of a double saucepan and carefully heat it, stirring all the time until it is thick enough to coat the back of your spoon – about the consistency of single cream. When this stage is reached pour the custard into a flameproof shallow dish, or into individual ramekin dishes. Stand the dish in a roasting tin half-filled with boiling water and put it into a moderately hot oven (200°C, 400°F, Gas Mark 6) long enough to form a good skin – if making one large one bake for 8 minutes, if making individual custards bake them for 7 minutes. Remove the custard and refrigerate, taking great care that the skin on the top is not broken.

Next day, not more than 3 hours before you are due to eat the crème brûlée, make the caramel top. Put the custard on a large sheet of greaseproof paper, or on a tray. Sift the castor sugar evenly all over the top to form a layer a little less than 5 mm/¼ inch deep.

Heat the grill and when blazing hot put the custard under it, as close as you can to the heat. Watch carefully. The sugar will first melt in bubbles, then slowly turn brown. You may need to turn the custard carefully so that you get an evenly browned top. As soon as the whole top is toffee remove the custard and allow it to cool. When stone cold the caramel on the top will be crackly and hard.

To serve the dish, crack the top with a serving spoon and give each diner some custard, which should be creamy and almost runny, and a piece of caramel.

SERVES FOUR

PINEAPPLE AND APRICOT CAKE

METRIC/IMPERIAL
4 thin slices fresh pineapple
100 g/4 oz fresh apricots, halved
3 eggs
75 g/3 oz castor sugar
finely grated rind of 1 lemon
1 teaspoon ground cinnamon
good pinch of salt
75 g/3 oz plain flour
150 ml/¼ pint double cream
1 tablespoon chopped brown almonds
few drops vanilla essence
2 teaspoons icing sugar
4 tablespoons apricot jam, sieved
FOR THE SYRUP
150 ml/¼ pint water
40 g/1½ oz granulated sugar

To make the syrup: put the water and the granulated sugar in a saucepan and bring slowly to the boil. Once the sugar has melted boil the syrup rapidly for a minute. Lower the temperature and put in the pineapple slices and the apricots. Poach slowly until the fruit is tender. Allow to cool.

Grease two 20–23-cm/8–9-inch sandwich tins and line with greaseproof paper. Set the oven to moderate (180°C, 350°F, Gas Mark 4). Whisk the eggs with the sugar using an electric beater (or set the bowl over a saucepan of simmering water to speed things up) until the mixture is thick, pale in colour, and very moussey. If beating over a hot saucepan, remove the bowl when the mixture is thick but continue beating until it is cold again.

Add the lemon rind, cinnamon and pinch of salt to the flour and fold into the egg mixture. Divide between the sandwich tins and spread flat with the back of a spoon or a spatula. Bake for 20 minutes. Allow the cakes to cool in the tins for 5 minutes, then turn out on a wire rack to cool.

Whip the double cream until thick and into it stir the chopped nuts, the vanilla essence and the icing sugar. Use this as a filling when you sandwich the completely cold cakes together.

Arrange the poached apricots and pineapple, without any syrup, on top of the cake. Heat the apricot jam in a saucepan, with as little stirring as possible, until it is runny. If still very thick add some of the poaching syrup. Brush or spoon the apricot jam over the fruit and allow to set.

SERVES FOUR TO SIX

COFFEE RUM HEDGEHOG

METRIC/IMPERIAL
2 plain sponge cakes
175 ml/6 fl oz water
50 g/2 oz brown sugar
3 heaped tablespoons instant coffee powder
1 tablespoon rum
75 g/3 oz butter
150 g/5 oz icing sugar
300 ml/½ pint double cream
50 g/2 oz whole or split blanched almonds

Break the cakes up roughly and put them in a bowl. Boil the water with the sugar and when the sugar is dissolved pour on to the coffee and mix well. Add the rum and pour over the cake. Mix with a fork or your hand, taking care not to mash the cake too much – you want a marbled half-white, half-brown effect. Then press the mixture into a pudding bowl and put a weight on top. (A saucer that fits inside the pudding bowl on top of the cake, with a large can of fruit on top will do nicely.) Leave for at least 3–4 hours, or overnight.

Meanwhile, make the butter icing: beat together the butter and the icing sugar until the mixture is very white and fluffy. Whip the cream until it is just firm enough to hold its shape. Brown the almonds in the oven or under the grill.

Turn the cake out on to a plate. Using a palette knife dipped in boiling water to help you, spread the butter icing evenly all over the surface of the cake. Then mask it with the whipped cream, and finally stick in the almonds, like the spikes of a hedgehog, all over the cake. The cake is very rich, so serve small helpings to start with.

SERVES SIX TO EIGHT

WALNUT AND LEMON MERINGUE CAKE

METRIC/IMPERIAL
4 egg whites
250 g/9 oz castor sugar
75 g/3 oz walnuts, chopped
300 ml/½ pint double cream
4 heaped tablespoons real lemon curd
(see Lemon Custard, page 136)

Line the bottom of two 20–23-cm/8–9-inch sandwich tins with rounds of greaseproof paper and brush them out with melted butter. Shake a little castor sugar round the sides and base to give an even coating.

Whisk the egg whites until stiff and fairly dry, then add half the castor sugar. Beat again until the mixture is smooth and sufficiently solid to hold its shape. Then add the rest of the sugar and beat again until once more it is very stiff and will hold its shape.

Stir most of the nuts (keeping back about a tablespoon) into the meringue mixture and divide it between the two sandwich tins. Spread evenly into the tins. Bake them in a moderately hot oven (190°C, 375°F, Gas Mark 5) for 40 minutes. Turn the cakes out on to a wire rack, peel off the paper and allow them to cool.

Whip the cream and mix half of it with the lemon curd. Sandwich the meringue cake with this mixture and use the rest of the cream to spread on the top. Lastly, sprinkle with the remainder of the nuts.

SERVES FOUR TO SIX

ALMOND MALAKOFF WITH RASPBERRIES OR STRAWBERRIES

METRIC/IMPERIAL
175 g/6 oz castor sugar
175 g/6 oz butter
300 ml/½ pint double cream
175 g/6 oz ground almonds
3 tablespoons Kirsch
225 g/8 oz fresh raspberries or strawberries
1 large packet boudoir biscuits

And simply extravagant. . .

Beat the sugar and butter with an electric mixer until really fluffy, soft and white. If you haven't a mixer there is nothing for it but to keep at it with a wooden spoon. Whip the cream until it is stiff enough to hold its shape. Add the ground almonds to it, then the Kirsch and finally the fruit (if using strawberries cut them in half when hulling them if they are large). Now mix the sugar and butter with the creamy fruit mixture.

Cut a circle of paper to fit the bottom of a straight-sided 18-cm/7-inch cake tin or a 1.5-litre/2½-pint soufflé dish. Put it in the tin and brush it well with oil. Line the sides of the cake tin or soufflé dish with a standing-up row of biscuits. Put their best-looking sides to the wall, so to speak. Spoon the malakoff mixture into the middle, pressing it down gently and smoothing the top. Refrigerate for at least 4 hours or until the malakoff feels firm.

With a serrated knife, or any really sharp knife, trim the tops of the sponge fingers so that they do not project above the level of the mixture. Turn the malakoff out, upside down, on to a serving plate and remove the circle of paper.

SERVES FOUR TO SIX

RASPBERRY BALUCHON

This is everything a sweet should be. Extravagantly rich in flavour but light enough to tackle at the end of dinner, with a tart, fresh, hot sauce. And spectacular enough to draw a gasp or two of admiration. It consists of crisp cups of biscuit, filled with ice cream, and served with a raspberry sauce. Not for beginners, as it requires timing and a bit of skill.

METRIC/IMPERIAL
FOR THE BISCUIT MIXTURE
75 g/3 oz butter
75 g/3 oz castor sugar
3 egg whites
75 g/3 oz plain flour, sifted
FOR THE ICE CREAM
600 ml/1 pint milk
225 g/8 oz sugar
1 vanilla pod
300 ml/½ pint single cream
8 egg yolks, beaten
100 g/4 oz chopped pistachio nuts
FOR THE SAUCE
3 whole eggs and 3 egg yolks
150 g/5 oz sugar
4 tablespoons framboise liqueur
350 g/12 oz fresh raspberries, sieved

To make the biscuit cups: melt the butter and add the sugar. Allow to cool. Gradually beat in the unwhisked egg whites, using a wire whisk. Fold in the sifted flour. Prepare two biscuit cups at a time. Spread 2 separate spoonfuls of mixture on a greased and floured baking tray, spreading very thinly and evenly with the back of a metal spoon to give two circles about 18 cm/7 inches in diameter. Bake in a hot oven (220°C, 425°F, Gas Mark 7) for 4 minutes. The biscuit should be just brown at the edges and pale in the middle.

While still hot and pliable, shape the discs of biscuit over an upturned jam jar, remove the jam jar when the paste has set slightly and gently squeeze the 'waist' of the pastry cup to give it a pretty shape. If you are making these before the party, let them cool, then store in an airtight polythene bag.

To make the ice cream: bring the milk, sugar, vanilla pod and single cream to the boil. Cool slightly, and pour on to the beaten yolks, stirring well. If the mixture is still very thin and runny, return it to a gentle heat and stir continuously until the custard will coat the back of the spoon. Immediately pour it into a cold bowl and allow to cool. Then add the nuts and freeze, either in an ice cream maker or in ice trays in the freezer, taking it out and whisking two or three times during the freezing process to prevent ice crystals forming.

When ready to serve, fill each baluchon with ice cream, stand it on a platter and put back in the coldest part of the refrigerator while you make the sauce. Whisk the whole eggs and yolks, sugar and liqueur together in a bowl. Then stand the bowl over a saucepan of simmering water and keep whisking. It will fluff up like Zabaglione. Stir in the sieved berries and serve with the ice creams.

SERVES FOUR TO SIX

CHOCOLATE CASE FILLED WITH TANGERINE MOUSSE

METRIC/IMPERIAL
FOR THE MOUSSE
3 whole eggs and 2 egg yolks
50 g/2 oz castor sugar
juice of ½ lemon
15 g/½ oz powdered gelatine
150 ml/¼ pint double cream
150 ml/¼ pint freshly squeezed tangerine juice
finely grated rind of 2 tangerines
FOR THE CASE
175 g/6 oz plain chocolate

You will need an 18-cm/7-inch paper baking case of the kind used for large cakes in bakeries.

To make the case: break up the chocolate and put it into a pudding basin. Stand this in or over simmering water and stir until the chocolate is smooth and melted, taking care that the chocolate does not over-heat – if it does it will look dull when cold. Using a clean pastry brush, paint the chocolate thinly over the inside of the paper case. Leave to cool and harden, and then repeat the process, again leaving it to harden. Repeat this until you have a thick layer and have used up all the chocolate. Refrigerate, and when hard carefully peel away the paper.

To make the mousse: put the eggs and the extra egg yolks with the sugar in a basin. Put it over a saucepan of simmering water, making sure that the bottom of the basin does not touch the water. Beat until the mixture is pale, thick and mousse-like. Remove from the heat and keep whisking until stone cold (if you have an electric beater the whisking need not be done over heat). Put the lemon juice plus 2 tablespoons of water into a small heavy saucepan. Sprinkle over the gelatine and leave to soak for 10 minutes.

Lightly whip the cream and stir it with the tangerine juice and the tangerine rind into the egg mixture.

Put the soaked gelatine over very gentle heat until it is completely clear and runny. Stir it briskly into the mousse mixture. Then carefully fill the chocolate case with the mixture and refrigerate until set.

SERVES FOUR TO SIX

PINEAPPLE WITH KIRSCH

This is such a simple recipe that I hesitate to include it, but it is an attractive way of presenting a fresh pineapple, and its simplicity does not detract from its excellence.

METRIC/IMPERIAL
1 large pineapple
icing sugar
Kirsch

Lay the pineapple down on a board. With a sharp knife cut off a slice from the top (which will include the leaves) and a slice from the bottom, which will enable the pineapple, when you have put it back together again, to stand up. Throw away the bottom slice. Using a sharp knife, cut the flesh out of the pineapple skin leaving the skin intact. This means working from both ends so that you extract a cylinder of fruit from the circle of skin. Try to keep the knife as close to the skin as possible without piercing it – the temptation to steer clear of the skin often means the inexperienced cook will dig too deeply into the fruit.

When you have loosened the flesh all round carefully push it out of the wider end. Slice the fruit very thinly across in rings. Stand the cylindrical pineapple skin on a serving dish with a good lip to it. Put back the pineapple slices sprinkling each one with half a teaspoon of Kirsch and a little icing sugar. Put back the pineapple top, leaves and all, and refrigerate well before serving.

SERVES FOUR TO SIX

And simply extravagant. . .

STRUDEL PASTRY

*Strudel pastry can be made at home quite easily, and indeed is fun to do.
But it is time consuming and ready-made strudel pastry leaves can be
bought from good German or Greek delicatessens. It is called variously
strudel pastry, filo pastry or baclava pastry. To make your own:*

METRIC/IMPERIAL
275 g/10 oz plain flour
good pinch of salt
1 small egg
150 ml/¼ pint water

Sift the flour and salt into a bowl. Mix the egg and water together and
whisk until smooth. Mix this liquid into the flour, adding more
water if necessary to make a soft dough. It should not be too sticky
when handled with a floured hand. Lift the whole mixture up in one
hand and then with a flick of the wrist throw it down on the table top
or on a board. Repeat this movement for about 10 minutes until the
pastry no longer sticks to your hands and the whole mixture is very
smooth and elastic.

Flour a bowl and put the pastry into it. Leave it for 15 minutes or
so by which time it will be ready for rolling and pulling. To do this,
flour the table top well and roll out the pastry as you would normal
pastry, but roll it until it is as thin as possible. Then flour one hand
and put it, palm side up, under the pastry. Use it to gently stretch
and pull the pastry until it is paper thin (you should be able to read
newsprint through it easily!). Keep pulling the pastry from all
directions, rolling the thick edges to get them thin too, until you
have a huge sheet of strudel pastry.

As soon as you have it at the required thinness cut off any
remaining thick edges and use at once. (It dries out very quickly and
will crack and become impossible to use). If you cannot use it
immediately, cover it well with a damp cloth or polythene wrapping
so that it cannot dry out. It can be frozen or kept refrigerated, but
the pieces should be well floured so that the folded layers do not stick
together, and the whole parcel must be well wrapped.

APPLE STRUDEL

METRIC/IMPERIAL

225 g/8 oz strudel pastry, rolled and pulled to about 60 by 30 cm/24
by 12 inches

flour for rolling

50–75 g/2–3 oz butter, melted

little oil

FOR THE FILLING

1 kg/2 lb cooking apples

1 tablespoon each currants, sultanas and raisins

1 tablespoon brown sugar

1 teaspoon ground cinnamon

finely grated rind and juice of 1 small lemon

3 tablespoons crushed digestive biscuits *or* browned dried
breadcrumbs

TO SERVE

icing sugar

whipped cream

Mix all the filling ingredients together. Flour a large piece of
sheeting or a tea towel and lay the rolled-out pastry on this. Brush it
all over with melted butter and add about a tablespoon of melted
butter to the filling ingredients too. Mix well and spread the filling all
over the buttered strudel pastry. Using the tea towel or cloth to help,
roll the strudel up keeping as close a roll as you can.

Brush a baking tray with oil. Lift the strudel carefully on to it and
brush again with melted butter. Bake in a moderately hot oven
(200°C, 400°F, Gas Mark 6) until golden brown – about 40 minutes.

Serve hot, dusted with icing sugar and cut across in thick slices.
Serve whipped cream separately.

SERVES FOUR TO SIX

And simply extravagant. . .

ORANGE AND GRAND MARNIER PANCAKES

METRIC/IMPERIAL
8 French pancakes (see page 36)
FOR THE CUSTARD
2 egg yolks
50 g/2 oz castor sugar
20 g/¾ oz flour
20 g/¾ oz cornflour
grated rind of 1 large orange
300 ml/½ pint milk
2 drops vanilla essence
2 tablespoons Grand Marnier
1 egg white
icing sugar

If you have not already done so make the French pancakes and keep them warm, well covered or wrapped in foil, in a very low oven.

To make the custard: mix together the egg yolks, the castor sugar, both the flours and the grated orange rind in the bottom of a saucepan. When well blended pour on the milk and put over a gentle heat. Stir constantly as you bring the mixture to the boil. It will go alarmingly lumpy but will eventually become thick and smooth. Draw it off the heat, add the vanilla essence and the Grand Marnier. Allow it to cool until warm rather than hot.

Whisk the egg white until stiff but not dry and fold it into the custard. Fill each pancake with a spoonful of this mixture, fold them loosely and put them on a flameproof serving dish. Sift over icing sugar fairly heavily.

Heat the grill until blazing hot and put the pancakes under it to turn the top to toffee. When bubbling and half browned, serve the pancakes.

To gild the lily thoroughly, why not pour a little Grand Marnier round the pancakes, set them alight, and serve with cream!

SERVES FOUR

TARTE DES DEMOISELLES TATIN

This is a sort of gourmet's Upside-Down Apple Cake.

METRIC/IMPERIAL
100 g/4 oz rich shortcrust pastry (see Mincemeat Flan, page 220)
about 50 g/2 oz butter
about 50 g/2 oz castor sugar
1 kg/2 lb good dessert apples
50 g/2 oz granulated suger
finely grated rind of ½ lemon

First make the pastry and put it, well wrapped, in the refrigerator to relax.

Grease an 18-cm/7-inch flan dish very thickly with the butter. Sprinkle with a deep layer of the castor sugar. Peel and core the apples and cut them into chunks. Pack them tightly into the flan dish, sprinkling a little more sugar as you go. Roll the pastry out and lay it on top of the apples, pressing the edges down firmly. Do not bother to decorate it – you are going to turn it upside down. Bake the pie in a moderately hot oven (200°C, 400°F, Gas Mark 6) for 30 minutes.

When the pie is cooked take it out and run a knife round the edge to make sure it is loose. Put a plate, upside down, on top of the pie and turn both plate and flan dish over together so that the pie ends up on the plate, apple side up. Ideally you should now have a toffee-like base to the cake, but if the apples were at all juicy it is unlikely that you have. For this reason you need to cheat a bit with a little extra toffee.

Put the granulated sugar into a heavy-bottomed saucepan and allow it to first melt and then turn to toffee over a very gentle heat. Once it has caramelised, sprinkle the apples with the grated lemon rind and pour over the runny caramel. Serve lukewarm.

SERVES FOUR

KING GEORGE CANNONBALL PLUM PUDDING

Plum puddings were once made of chopped meat (usually beef with plenty of suet), fruit (including plums), and spices. They were known as mincemeat puddings or plum puddings, and were wrapped in a cloth to be boiled suspended in a cauldron of water over the fire. Gradually they became more sweet than savoury and, by Georgian times, were puddings as we know them, but still boiled in the traditional cloth. I think the ball shape much prettier than the pudding-basin shape, but if you prefer to stick to a basin this recipe will make two 1.15-litre/2-pint puds. If you want a cannonball you will need a pudding cloth (or a piece of sheet) and a heavy-duty (freezing-type) polythene bag.

METRIC/IMPERIAL
100 g/4 oz prunes
300 ml/½ pint beer
grated rind and juice of 1 lemon *or* ½ orange
2 tablespoons black treacle
3 eggs
4 tablespoons rum
100 g/4 oz self-raising flour
225 g/8 oz shredded suet
225 g/8 oz fresh white breadcrumbs
350 g/12 oz soft brown sugar
50 g/2 oz flaked almonds
225 g/8 oz seedless raisins
225 g/8 oz currants
225 g/8 oz sultanas
100 g/4 oz chopped mixed peel
½ teaspoon mixed spice
½ teaspoon ground nutmeg
½ teaspoon ground cinnamon
pinch of salt

Essentially what you do is mix the wet ingredients into the dry ingredients. So: first soak the prunes in the beer until soft enough to stone and chop them. Add the grated rind and juice from the orange or lemon to the beer and prunes. Heat the treacle until runny and add that too, then mix in the eggs and rum.

In a big bowl mix all the dry ingredients together, then stir the liquid in very thoroughly. Using a hand is easier than wielding a wooden spoon.

Butter the polythene bag. Turn it buttered-side in. Fill with the pudding mixture and tie the top with string. Tie the whole thing in the cloth, like Dick Whittington's bag. Suspend the pud in a large pan of boiling water so that the whole pud is submerged but not touching the bottom. (A deep preserving pan with a fixed handle to tie the cloth strings to is good, or a really large saucepan with a wooden spoon across the top to tie the strings to will do, or you may be able to suspend the pud from the grill rack.) Make sure there are no bits of cloth or string hanging over the gas flames or hotplate – the pudding will be boiling for hours, some of which time you will not be in the kitchen to watch it and you don't want a conflagration.

Boil gently but steadily for 10 hours, topping up the pan with boiling water as necessary. Cool the pudding in the suspended position, with the water poured away (if you put it on a plate it will have a flat bottom).

When cold, unwrap and peel off the polythene bag (which may have burst but it doesn't matter) and put the pudding into a clean unbuttered bag for storage.

To reheat, butter the bag as before, and boil as before, this time for 3 hours. Serve the pudding with a sprig of holly and flame with brandy.

NOTE The trick to successful flaming is to *slightly* warm the brandy before lighting it, and to light it before you pour – while it is still in the ladle or saucepan. Don't overheat the liquor or you will lose it all by evaporation and the flames will be frighteningly high. If the holly is fresh the fire makes it crackle marvellously, like Chinese firecrackers, but you may have to stop it burning after a minute or two – burning holly doesn't smell too good, and is mildly poisonous!

SERVES SIX

BOXING DAY CHRISTMAS PUDDING

Cut left-over plum pudding into 1-cm/½-inch slices. Sugar both sides of the slices, pressing the sugar in well. Fry them in hot butter in a heavy frying pan and serve at once with brandy butter, or Passionfruit Sauce, or whipped cream.

And simply extravagant. . .

PASSIONFRUIT SAUCE FOR CHRISTMAS PUDDING

This is highly untraditional, but delicious especially with Boxing Day's fried Christmas pudding. It also makes a good dinner-party sweet on its own, served in individual cups and dishes.

METRIC/IMPERIAL
150 ml/¼ pint passionfruit pulp
1 tablespoon sherry
castor sugar
300 ml/½ pint double cream, half whipped

Mix the fruit with the sherry and sugar to taste and stir into the cream.

SERVES FOUR

MINCEMEAT FLAN

METRIC/IMPERIAL
FOR THE PASTRY
175 g/6 oz plain flour
pinch of salt
90 g/3½ oz butter
1 egg yolk
2 tablespoons icy water
squeeze of lemon juice
FOR THE FILLING
75 g/3 oz beef suet, chopped
75 g/3 oz raisins
75 g/3 oz sultanas
1 small dessert apple
75 g/3 oz brown sugar
75 g/3 oz currants
40 g/1½ oz chopped mixed peel
40 g/1½ oz chopped almonds
grated rind of ½ lemon
pinch of mixed spice
1 tablespoon brandy

Make the pastry first. Sift the flour with the salt and rub in the butter until the mixture looks like breadcrumbs. Mix the yolk and 1 tablespoon of the water with the lemon juice and mix this into the flour with a knife. Then use one hand to press it to a firm dough. Add more water if necessary, but do not make the pastry too damp.

Roll it out and use it to line an 18-cm/7-inch flan ring or flan dish. Reserve any pastry trimmings for later. Prick all over and line with a double piece of greaseproof paper, then fill it with dried beans, rice, pebbles or pennies.

Set the oven to moderately hot (200°C, 400°F, Gas Mark 6) and leave it to heat for 15 minutes while the pastry case relaxes in the refrigerator. When the oven is hot bake the flan case until just beginning to brown round the edges. Then take out the paper and the 'blind' beans and return the pastry case to the oven for 5–10 minutes to dry out completely. Cool on a wire rack.

To make the mincemeat, simply mix all the filling ingredients together and put them through a mincer. Fill the flan with the mincemeat. Use the pastry trimmings to make a fine lattice, sticking the ends with a little water. Brush the pastry strips with a very little water and sprinkle with castor sugar. Return to the oven for 10–15 minutes, or until pastry strips are cooked.

Serve lukewarm with whipped cream.

SERVES FOUR

Vegetables

Vegetables

BROAD BEANS WITH BACON

This is extravagant as only the bright green middle of each bean is used.
But it's good enough to serve as a course on its own.

METRIC/IMPERIAL
1 kg/2 lb fresh unshelled broad beans per person
1 rasher streaky bacon per person
1 tablespoon chopped fresh thyme
salt and pepper

Shell the beans and boil them in salted water for 6–7 minutes or until
just tender. Dunk immediately into cold water and cool them
rapidly. Peel off the bluish outer skins.

Remove the bacon rind and chop up the bacon. Fry it slowly in a
pan until crisp but not brittle. Just before serving add the beans,
chopped thyme, salt and pepper and shake the pan until the beans
are hot.

SERVES FOUR

CABBAGE WITH CARAWAY

METRIC/IMPERIAL
1 medium cabbage
25 g/1 oz butter, melted
salt and freshly ground black pepper
lemon juice
caraway seeds
2–3 tablespoons soured cream

Shred the cabbage and boil in plenty of fast-boiling water for 2–3 minutes or until just tender. Drain well. Toss immediately in melted butter, adding salt, pepper, lemon juice, and caraway seeds to taste. Put into a serving dish and fork in the soured cream.

SERVES FOUR

PETITS POIS À LA FRANÇAISE

Here is the classic Petits Pois à la Française. It doesn't look quite as glamorous as the second recipe, but it tastes too good for glamour to matter.

METRIC/IMPERIAL
large sprig of mint
2 or 3 parsley stalks
1 kg/2 lb shelled fresh peas
1 large mild onion, very finely sliced
1 medium lettuce, finely shredded
4 or 5 tablespoons water
50 g/2 oz butter
1 teaspoon sugar
½ teaspoon salt
freshly ground black pepper

Tie the herbs together with a piece of string and put them in the bottom of a shallow ovenproof dish, large enough to hold the other ingredients. Put everything together into this and cover with greaseproof paper or foil. Put into a moderate oven (180°C, 350°F, Gas Mark 4) for 1½–2 hours, or until the peas are nearly tender. Remove the herbs before serving.

If you want to thicken the liquid that will have run from the peas, mix together a teaspoon each of flour and butter. Lift the peas and other ingredients out of the dish and put them in a fresh serving dish. Now whisk a little flour and butter paste into the liquid, while bringing it gradually to the boil. Whisk in little bits at a time, stopping when the liquid is sufficiently thickened.

SERVES FOUR

SPEEDY PETITS POIS À LA FRANÇAISE

METRIC/IMPERIAL
1 (227-g/8-oz) packet frozen peas
50 g/2 oz butter
1 onion, finely sliced
6 or 7 lettuce leaves, finely shredded
1 teaspoon chopped mint
salt and freshly ground black pepper

Boil the frozen peas in salted water and drain well. Melt the butter in a frying pan and cook the onion until soft and just beginning to brown. Add the lettuce leaves and stir until they are reduced and soft. Fork this mixture, butter and all, into the cooked peas and sprinkle with the mint and freshly ground black pepper. Add more salt if needed.

SERVES FOUR

ROAST PARSNIPS

Parsnips can take longer to roast than the meat with which they are to be served. For this reason I generally boil them for a few minutes first.

METRIC/IMPERIAL
675 g/1½ lb peeled parsnips, cut in half lengthways
50 g/2 oz melted butter
2 teaspoons runny honey
salt and pepper

Set the oven to moderately hot (200°C, 400°F, Gas Mark 6). Boil the parsnips in salted water for 10 minutes, then drain them. Melt the butter in a roasting tin and turn the parsnips in this. Pour over the honey and sprinkle with salt and pepper.

Roast in the oven, basting and turning occasionally until brown and tender – about 20 minutes, depending on the size of the parsnips.

If you are roasting the parsnips without boiling them first, do not add the honey until the last 15 minutes or so for fear that it will burn. The parsnips may need as much as 2 hours in the oven.

SERVES FOUR

MASHED PARSNIPS

METRIC/IMPERIAL
450 g/1 lb parsnips
75 g/3 oz butter
1 small clove garlic, crushed (optional)
2 teaspoons lemon juice
salt and pepper
450 g/1 lb mashed potato

Peel the parsnips and slice them very finely. Melt the butter in the
bottom of a heavy saucepan and put in the parsnips, crushed garlic
and lemon juice. Season with salt and pepper and cover the pan with
a well-fitting lid. Cook very gently until the parsnips are mushy.
Then remove the lid and using a potato masher beat the parsnips to a
pulp. Whip in the mashed potato and reheat.

SERVES FOUR

CARROTS WITH GINGER

METRIC/IMPERIAL
1 kg/2 lb carrots
melted butter
1–2 teaspoons sugar
good pinch of ground ginger
salt and freshly ground black pepper

Peel the carrots and boil them in salted water until just tender. Then
drain them and toss in a little melted butter with a teaspoon or so of
sugar and a good pinch of ginger. Cook them, shaking the pan
frequently until the carrots are just beginning to brown at the edges.
Tip into a serving dish and grind over a little black pepper.

SERVES FOUR

MARROW WITH MUSHROOMS

*This is a good, light recipe with no calories to speak of — but unfortunately
it must be served promptly as it loses colour on standing.*

METRIC/IMPERIAL
225 g/8 oz young marrow
225 g/8 oz mushrooms
lemon juice
salt and freshly ground black pepper

Slice the marrows, skin and all, as finely as you can. Slice the
mushrooms. Put both marrow and mushroom into a heavy saucepan
with a good squeeze of lemon. Cover with a lid. Cook over a low
heat, shaking the pan gently until the vegetables are cooked but not
mushy. Add plenty of salt and black pepper to taste.

SERVES FOUR

RED CABBAGE

METRIC/IMPERIAL
50 g/2 oz butter
1 onion, coarsely chopped
1 kg/2 lb red cabbage, fairly finely shredded
1 cooking apple, peeled and sliced
2 dessert apples, peeled and sliced
1 tablespoon sultanas
2 teaspoons brown sugar
2 teaspoons vinegar
pinch of ground cloves
salt and pepper
250 ml/8 fl oz water

Use a very large saucepan with a heavy base. In it melt the butter and
fry the chopped onion until it begins to soften. Then add everything
else with the water and stir well. Cover tightly with a really well-
fitting lid and cook slowly, giving the pan an occasional stir, for 1½
hours or until the whole mass is very soft and reduced in bulk. Take
care that the bottom does not catch and burn. Just before serving,
taste and add more salt, pepper, vinegar or sugar as necessary.

SERVES FOUR TO SIX

TOMATO CLAMART

METRIC/IMPERIAL
4–6 tomatoes
50 g/2 oz butter
1 onion, sliced
1 clove garlic, crushed
450 g/1 lb shelled fresh peas or frozen peas
1 teaspoon chopped mint
salt and pepper

Dip the tomatoes in boiling water for 5 seconds, then skin them. Cut a good slice off the rounded end of each one, and scoop the flesh and seeds from the centre. Keep both cups and lids of tomato.

Melt 40 g/1½ oz of the butter and in it fry the onion until just coloured. Add the crushed garlic and fry a further minute.

Boil the peas in salted water until just tender then drain well. Put the peas, onion and butter mixture, mint, and plenty of salt and pepper into an electric blender or vegetable mouli and mix to a smooth purée. Fill the tomatoes with this mixture, and put back the lids at a jaunty angle.

Use the rest of the butter to grease an ovenproof dish and to brush the top of each tomato. Put them into a moderately hot oven (200°C, 400°F, Gas Mark 6) until the tomato cases are just soft and the pea filling hot. Take care not to overcook.

SERVES FOUR

NOODLES WITH BASIL

METRIC/IMPERIAL
225 g/8 oz noodles
40 g/1½ oz butter
1 clove garlic, crushed
salt and freshly ground black pepper
2 teaspoons fresh basil, chopped

Boil the noodles in plenty of salted water for 10–15 minutes or until they are tender, but not mushy. Drain them and rinse under the tap to remove any excess starch. Return them to the saucepan with the butter, garlic, salt and pepper, and basil. Shake over the heat until hot.

SERVES FOUR

CREAMED CELERIAC

METRIC/IMPERIAL
225 g/8 oz celeriac
300 ml/½ pint creamy milk
2 large potatoes
50 g/2 oz butter
salt and white pepper

Wash the celeriac, peel it and slice it finely. Put it in a pan with the milk and simmer until tender (about 30 minutes). Meanwhile, peel the potatoes and boil them in salted water until tender.

Liquidise the celeriac with its milk until smooth. Drain the potatoes and return them to the heat. Mash well, allowing them to dry off thoroughly. Now beat into them the celeriac, with any remaining milk, and the butter. Add salt and pepper to taste.

SERVES FOUR

VEGETABLE MORNAY

METRIC/IMPERIAL
1 small cauliflower
225 g/8 oz shelled peas *or* 1 (227-g/8-oz) packet frozen peas
450 g/1 lb carrots
3 tomatoes
600 ml/1 pint milk
40 g/1½ oz butter
40 g/1½ oz flour
salt and white pepper
65 g/2½ oz cheese (preferably strong Cheddar *or*
Gruyère), finely grated

Wash the cauliflower and break it into sprigs. Boil it in salt water until just tender, but not really soft. Drain well. Cook the peas and drain them. Peel and slice the carrots and boil them too, again taking care not to get them too soft. Plunge the tomatoes into boiling water for 5 seconds, peel them and cut into quarters. Do not cook them further.

Mix all the vegetables in a flameproof dish and then make the sauce:

In a heavy saucepan, melt the butter and stir in the flour. Cook, stirring, for 1 minute or until the butter is foaming. Draw the pan off the heat and slowly add the milk, stirring as you go. Once the mixture is smooth bring it to a rolling boil, then lower the heat and simmer for 2 minutes. Draw the pan off the heat again, season the sauce with salt and pepper and stir in all but a tablespoon of the cheese.

Once the cheese has melted, pour the sauce all over the vegetables and sprinkle on the rest of the cheese. Put the dish into a hot oven (220°C, 425°F, Gas Mark 7) or under the grill, to reheat and slightly brown the top.

SERVES FOUR TO SIX

POTATO CAKE (ROSTI POTATOES)

METRIC/IMPERIAL
50 g/2 oz bacon dripping *or* butter
1 large onion, sliced
1 kg/2 lb large floury potatoes, peeled
salt and pepper
1 egg, beaten

Melt half the bacon dripping or butter in a frying pan and cook the onion until soft and just beginning to brown.

Boil the potatoes for 7 minutes or until half cooked. Grate, while still hot, into a bowl. Season with salt and pepper and add the egg, cooked onion and fat.

Melt the rest of the bacon dripping in the frying pan and in it cook large tablespoons of the potato mixture, formed into flat small potato cakes. Cook the mixture slowly so that the potato has time to cook through. When browned on the underside, carefully turn over to brown the other side.

SERVES FOUR TO SIX

BAKED POTATOES STUFFED WITH CHEESE AND ONION

METRIC/IMPERIAL
4 large baking potatoes
about 40 g/1½ oz butter
75 g/3 oz Gruyère cheese, cut into small dice
1 large Spanish onion, sliced
salt and pepper

Wash the potatoes and prick them all over. Dust them with salt and bake in a moderately hot oven (200°C, 400°F, Gas Mark 6) until they are soft right through – about 1½ hours for medium potatoes, 1¾ hours for large ones.

Meanwhile melt the butter in a frying pan and cook the sliced onion until soft and just beginning to brown.

When the potatoes are cooked take them out, split them in half and scoop out the potato flesh. With a fork mix it with the onion and any butter from the pan, and add salt and pepper as necessary. Lastly add the diced cheese, mix quickly and pile back into the 8 potato halves. Brush the tops with melted butter and return to the oven to melt the cheese.

SERVES FOUR

DAUPHINOISE POTATOES

METRIC/IMPERIAL
450 g/1 lb potatoes, peeled
butter
salt and pepper
grated nutmeg
2 tablespoons cream
about 200 ml/7 fl oz creamy milk
1 egg, beaten
1 tablespoon dried white breadcrumbs

Slice the potatoes as finely as you can and slip them into cold water as you do so (this is not strictly necessary, but it helps to prevent discoloration, and washes off some of the starchiness which would make the final dish sticky. But if you like the stickiness – and many people do – don't put them in water.)

Butter a shallow pie-dish. Drain the potatoes if they have been in water, and layer them in the pie dish, sprinkling with salt, pepper and nutmeg as you go. Mix the cream and milk with the beaten egg and season with salt and pepper. Pour this over the potatoes and sprinkle with the crumbs. Put a few blobs of butter on the top and bake in a moderate oven (180°C, 350°F, Gas Mark 4) until the top is brown and crisp, and the potatoes are soft right through.

SERVES FOUR

RATATOUILLE

METRIC/IMPERIAL
2 small aubergines, sliced
4 tomatoes
salad oil
olive oil
1 large onion, sliced
1 clove garlic, crushed
2 medium courgettes, sliced
1 small red pepper, sliced
1 medium green pepper, sliced
salt and freshly ground black pepper
½ teaspoon crushed coriander
3 or 4 basil leaves, chopped

Put the sliced aubergines on a plate and sprinkle with salt. After 20 minutes rinse them well and dry thoroughly.

Plunge the tomatoes into boiling water for 5 seconds, then peel and quarter them. Put 2 tablespoons salad oil and 1 tablespoon olive oil into a frying pan and add the onion. Cook slowly until soft, then add the garlic. Cook for a further minute and lift out the onions with a perforated spoon. Put them into a saucepan.

Now fry the aubergine slices until brown on both sides, adding more oil if you need to. Lift them out and add to the onion. Then treat the courgettes the same way. Put the peppers, both red and green, into the saucepan with the onion, aubergines and courgettes and put on a well-fitting lid. Simmer gently for 25 minutes or until everything is soft and bordering on the mushy. Add the tomato pieces, season with salt and plenty of freshly ground black pepper. Add the coriander and boil rapidly for 10 minutes to allow most of the juices to evaporate.

If serving the ratatouille hot, tip it into a serving dish and sprinkle with the chopped basil. If serving cold, chill first and sprinkle over the chopped basil just before serving.

SERVES FOUR

Salads

Salads

TABOULI

This is a Middle Eastern salad made with cracked wheat, parsley and lemon. Cracked wheat is sold in specialist shops under the name Burghul or, sometimes, Bourghul.

METRIC/IMPERIAL
100 g/4 oz fine cracked wheat
1 tomato
½ cucumber
good handful of fresh parsley
5 leaves fresh mint
2 shallots
3 or 4 tablespoons olive oil
lemon juice
salt and pepper

Soak the cracked wheat for about 1 hour in cold water. It will swell up. Drain it and squeeze it dry in a clean tea towel. Then spread the wheat out on a tray to dry further while you get on with the rest.

Dip the tomato into boiling water for 5 seconds to make it easy to skin. Peel it and cut into quarters, discarding the seeds. Chop it up. Chop the cucumber (the skin too), and chop the parsley as finely as you can. Chop the mint and the shallots. (All this chopping can be done in a machine, but take great care that the result is chopped and not liquidised.)

Mix all the ingredients together, adding plenty of lemon juice, salt and pepper.

SERVES FOUR

SPINACH SALAD WITH BACON AND YOGURT

METRIC/IMPERIAL
4 rashers streaky bacon, with rind removed
450 g/1 lb fresh young spinach leaves, with stalks removed
FOR THE DRESSING
2 tablespoons plain yogurt
2 tablespoons double cream
2 tablespoons oil (preferably olive)
½ tablespoon vinegar or lemon juice
1 teaspoon French mustard
1 clove garlic, crushed
½ teaspoon sugar
salt and freshly ground black pepper

Grill the bacon until really crisp. Chop it and allow to cool on absorbent kitchen paper so that it is not greasy. Wash the spinach leaves and dry them thoroughly.

Mix all the ingredients for the dressing together, shaking well in a screw-top jar, or putting them together in an electric blender. Pour the dressing all over the spinach and mix well. Tip into a salad bowl and scatter over the bacon bits.

SERVES FOUR

MINT AND CARROT SALAD

METRIC/IMPERIAL
3 tablespoons salad oil
1 tablespoon wine vinegar
salt and pepper
1 teaspoon curry powder
1 kg/2 lb carrots, peeled
2 tablespoons chopped mint

Put the oil, vinegar, salt, pepper and curry powder into a screw-top jar and shake well.

Using a potato peeler shred the carrots into very fine ribbons, or grate them coarsely. Mix them with the mint and the dressing and toss well.

SERVES FOUR TO SIX

MUSHROOM AND PRAWN SALAD

If the salad is to form the main course of a light meal instead of being served as a starter, increase the quantities to 350 g/12 oz each of mushrooms and prawns.

METRIC/IMPERIAL
175 g/6 oz button mushrooms, sliced
175 g/6 oz fresh cooked peeled prawns
FOR THE DRESSING
4 tablespoons salad oil
2 tablespoons olive oil
1 tablespoons lemon juice
1 tablespoon white wine vinegar
1 small clove garlic, crushed
1 tablespoon finely chopped mint
1 teaspoon finely chopped parsley
salt and freshly ground black pepper

Mix the dressing ingredients together, or shake them in a screw-top jar. Toss the mushrooms in this, and leave for 6 hours to marinate. Mix in the prawns and tip into a serving dish.

SERVES FOUR

CELERY, SWEET CORN AND PINEAPPLE SALAD

METRIC/IMPERIAL
1 small pineapple *or* a few slices of canned pineapple, well drained
2 sticks celery
1 (198-g/7-oz) can sweet corn *or* 1 (227-g/8-oz) packet frozen sweet corn
2 tablespoons flaked almonds
3 tablespoons salad oil (not olive oil)
1 teaspoon lemon juice
2 teaspoons wine vinegar
good pinch of salt
freshly ground black pepper

Cut the pineapple into small pieces, and chop the celery. Drain the sweet corn if it is canned. If it is frozen boil it until tender in salted

241

water, drain it and rinse under cold water to cool. Then dry well.

Put the pineapple, almonds, celery and sweet corn in a bowl and mix with all the other ingredients.

SERVES FOUR TO SIX

BEAN AND PEA SALAD

METRIC/IMPERIAL
100 g/4 oz dried haricot beans
100 g/4 oz red kidney beans
100 g/4 oz dried chick peas
6 tablespoons salad oil
1½ tablespoons wine vinegar
salt and pepper
1 tablespoon chopped parsley
½ teaspoon made French mustard
2 teaspoons chopped mint
1 dozen black olives (optional)

Soak the beans and peas in separate bowls in cold water overnight, or for 3–4 hours in warm water, until they are plumped up and slightly softened. Then boil them in separate pans in salted water for 1–2 hours, until they are tender but not broken up. Rinse them under cold water and dry well. Put them into 3 separate bowls.

Mix the oil, vinegar, salt and pepper together and shake in a screw-top jar until well emulsified. Pour a third of the dressing into each bowl and then add the parsley to the haricot beans, the mustard to the red kidney beans and the mint to the chick peas. Make sure the mustard is well distributed.

Dish the pulses in 3 small piles on a serving dish and garnish with the black olives.

SERVES FOUR TO SIX

Salads

BEETROOT, ONION AND SOURED CREAM SALAD

METRIC/IMPERIAL
1 (142-ml/5-fl oz) carton soured cream
1 teaspoon horseradish cream *or* horseradish sauce
1 teaspoon lemon juice
salt and freshly ground black pepper
675 g/1½ lb cooked beetroot
1 mild Spanish onion, finely sliced
3 or 4 spring onions, chopped

Mix together the soured cream, the horseradish sauce and the lemon juice, and season with salt and plenty of pepper.

Slice the beetroot into a serving dish and as you do so sprinkle in the onion slices. Pour or spoon the sauce over the top. Sprinkle on the chopped spring onions.

SERVES FOUR TO SIX

ALMOST-WALDORF SALAD

METRIC/IMPERIAL
2 cloves garlic, crushed
2 tablespoons olive oil
2 or 3 anchovy fillets, finely chopped
2 tablespoons lemon juice
good pinch of dry English mustard
1 egg
freshly ground black pepper
2 slices white bread, with crusts removed
Webb's Wonder lettuce (or other very crisp lettuce), washed, drained and broken up
3 or 4 tablespoons finely grated Parmesan cheese

Mix the crushed garlic with the olive oil. Take two-thirds of it and mix it with the chopped anchovy, lemon juice, mustard and raw egg. Whisk well or blend in an electric blender. Season with plenty of freshly ground black pepper.

Cut the bread into small dice and put the remaining garlicky olive oil into a frying pan. Heat the oil slowly and when the garlic shreds begin to sizzle, add the diced bread and fry until crisp and brown, turning frequently with a spoon. Cool the croûtons on absorbent paper and when stone cold add to the lettuce leaves.

Just before serving, toss the lettuce in the dressing and add the grated cheese.

SERVES FOUR TO SIX

FRILLY BITTER SALAD

You will need any or all of the following slightly bitter salad leaves. The only one that is essential is the curly endive (which should constitute the main ingredient of the salad).

METRIC/IMPERIAL
1 curly endive
1 bunch watercress
1 head chicory
few sprigs of young kale
few leaves of young spinach
1 lamb's lettuce
FOR THE DRESSING
3 tablespoons salad oil
1 tablespoon olive oil
1 tablespoon wine vinegar
½ clove garlic, crushed (optional)
1 teaspoon French mustard
salt and freshly ground black pepper

Simply wash the leaves carefully and shake them as dry as you can. Put the dressing ingredients into a screw-top jar, shake until they are well emulsified, pour over the salad, and turn until all the leaves are coated.

SERVES SIX TO EIGHT

ITALIAN PASTA SALAD

METRIC/IMPERIAL

100 g/4 oz shell-shaped pasta
1 (340-g/12-oz) can flageolet beans
½ large Spanish onion, finely sliced
1 (198-g/7-oz) can tuna fish
1 teaspoon chopped basil
1 teaspoon chopped parsley
2 tablespoons salad oil
2 teaspoons wine vinegar
2 teaspoons lemon juice
salt and freshly ground black pepper
mustard and cress
black olives

Bring a large pan of salted water to the boil. Drop in the pasta and boil for 10 minutes, stirring occasionally. The pasta should by then be just tender, but by no means mushy. Drain and rinse under cold water to remove any excess starch. Drain again, turning the pasta shells occasionally to make sure they dry completely.

Tip the flageolet beans into a colander or sieve and run cold water through them to remove the starchy liquid. Drain them well and then put into a bowl with the sliced onion and the tuna fish (plus the oil from the can). Add the pasta, the chopped herbs and the oil, vinegar and lemon juice. Add salt if needed, and plenty of freshly ground black pepper. Be careful not to stir the salad too much or the tuna will break up, making the dish look unattractive and soggy.

Turn the salad into a serving dish, snip some mustard and cress over the top and sprinkle with black olives.

SERVES FOUR

SALAD NIÇOISE

This salad is really best done for a largish party, or as a main course for fewer people. This is because the best Niçoise has all the listed ingredients in it. But naturally it does not have to contain the lot.

METRIC/IMPERIAL

6 or 8 young radishes, washed
black olives
3 tomatoes, skinned and quartered
2 hard-boiled eggs, quartered lengthwise
1 small Spanish onion, finely sliced
1 small green pepper, seeded and finely sliced
225 g/8 oz cooked French beans
1 (198-g/7-oz) can tuna fish
5 or 6 anchovy fillets, split lengthwise
handful of very fresh crisp lettuce leaves

FOR THE DRESSING

2 tablespoons olive oil
2 teaspoons red wine vinegar
1 small clove garlic, crushed
1 good tablespoon finely chopped fresh herbs (e.g. tarragon, basil, marjoram)
salt and freshly ground black pepper

Do not cut all the green part from the radishes, but leave a short stalk. Trim off the roots. Stone the olives. Put aside a few black olives, quarters of tomato, hard-boiled eggs, and radishes for the top of the salad and put everything else into a large bowl.

Mix together the oil, vinegar, garlic and herbs, and season well with salt and pepper. Toss the salad ingredients in this dressing and then tip the salad into a clean bowl. Put the reserved olives, radishes, egg, etc. on top of the salad, and serve.

SERVES FOUR TO SIX

FOUR BEAN SALAD

METRIC/IMPERIAL
1 (340-g/12-oz) can flageolet beans
1 (213-g/7½-oz) can butter beans *or* 225 g/8 oz boiled butter beans
225 g/8 oz fresh French beans
2 tablespoons flaked almonds
1 tablespoon olive oil
3 tablespoons salad oil
1 tablespoon red wine vinegar
1 tablespoon mixed chopped chives, parsley and mint
1 small clove garlic, crushed
salt and pepper
225 g/8 oz broad beans, cooked

Drain the canned beans well and rinse the flageolets under cold water to remove the starchy liquid. Boil the French beans in salted water until just tender, drain them and rinse under cold water to set the colour.

Fry the almonds in the olive oil until they are just beginning to brown. Allow them to cool. Mix together, in a screw-top jar or bowl, the oils, vinegar, herbs and garlic, and season well with salt and pepper. Shake or whisk until well emulsified and pour over all the beans.

Turn the beans in the dressing, tip them into a serving dish and scatter over the fried almonds.

SERVES SIX

CABBAGE WITH LEMON DRESSING

METRIC/IMPERIAL
450 g/1 lb hard white cabbage
1 tablespoon lemon juice
finely grated rind of 1 small lemon
1 tablespoon olive oil
salt and freshly ground black pepper
pinch of sugar
3 tablespoons double cream

Shred the cabbage as finely as you can. Mix all the remaining ingredients together, adding the cream last. Taste and adjust the seasoning if necessary. Using your hand (which is much more effective than a spoon) mix the dressing into the cabbage thoroughly. Tip into a clean salad bowl.

SERVES FOUR TO SIX

POTATO SALAD

This is a particularly good potato salad, and if mixed with chopped or sliced frankfurters, ham or salami, makes a very good lunch-time dish.

METRIC/IMPERIAL
675 g/1½ lb small firm potatoes
large sprig of mint
2 tablespoons salad oil
2 teaspoons wine vinegar
3 tablespoons soured cream
1 tablespoon mayonnaise
2 tablespoons chopped chives

Do not peel the potatoes but wash them well. Boil them in salted water, with the sprig of mint, until just tender. Peel them while they are still hot. Cut them up if they are at all large. While they are still hot mix them well with the oil and the vinegar. Leave them to cool.

Mix the soured cream, mayonnaise and half the chives together and turn the potatoes in this dressing. Turn them into a clean salad bowl and sprinkle with the rest of the chopped chives.

SERVES FOUR

Index

Index

Index

Index

Index

Index